OPEN ADOPTION

Also by Jeanne Warren Lindsay

Teens Look at Marriage:
Rainbows, Roles and Reality

Teenage Marriage: Coping with Reality

Teens Parenting:
The Challenge of Babies and Toddlers

Pregnant Too Soon: Adoption Is an Option

Do I Have A Daddy?
A Story About a Single-Parent Child

OPEN ADOPTION
A CARING OPTION

by Jeanne Warren Lindsay

Morning
Glory
Press

Buena Park, California

First Edition

Library of Congress Cataloging-in-Publication Data

Lindsay, Jeanne Warren.
    Open adoptions.

    Bibliography: p.
    Includes index.
    1. Adoption—United States—Case studies. 2. Adoptive
    parents—United States—Case studies. 3. Adoptees —
    United States—Case studies. 4. Children, Adopted—
    United States—Case studies. I. Title.
HV875.55.L55 1987   362.7'34'0973   86-21807
ISBN 0-930934-22-9
ISBN 0-930934-23-7 (pbk.)

MORNING GLORY PRESS
6595 San Haroldo Way   Buena Park, CA 90620
Telephone (714) 828-1998

*To the Birthparents and Adoptive Parents
Who Share So Generously
Their Stories
and
Their Love for Their Children*

Contents

Open adoption offers choices; Interviews provide data;
Legal aspects of adoption; High cost of adoption;
Difficulties of choosing.

Three different scripts; Defining open adoption;
Reasons for closed adoption; Agency versus
independent adoption; Trying a different way;
Adoption is changing; Sonia's story; Postscript; Chris
and Colette's experience.

Not all clients choose adoption; Openness developed
over time; Birthparents/Adoptive parents form
relationship; Counseling is crucial; Home studies are
extensive; Mystical bonds of open adoption; Leann's
story; Caring counselor at Options; Instant bond with
adoptive parents; Leann's mother shares feelings;
Mary and Toby's experience; "You have a new son
to meet."

Open adoption in early history; Adoption legislation
in the United States; Sealed records become law; "I
was sent away"; Search movement affects adoption;
Positive effects of reunion; Elaine and John choose
secrecy; Sara's feelings about adoption; Another
birthmother's story; Bridgit decides on adoption;
Adoptive parents refuse contact.

offered; Denise's story; DeeDee and Rick adopt
again; What about the risk?

   Many infants placed independently; Counseling may
   be lacking; Mature decisions needed in open
   adoption; Adoptive parents may object; Does
   confidentiality provide protection? An almost-
   disrupted adoption; Veronica's story; Value of
   counseling.

    Founder is adoptive parent; State licensed agency;
    Consideration of open adoption; Choosing a family;
    Mediation agreement developed; Counseling for
    adoptive couples, Wanda Sue's story; Sally and
    Stewart become parents.

    Closed adoption six years ago; Contact with first
    adoptive father; Second time — completely different;
    Adoption agreement developed; Bernardo's
    experiences; Jim and Janice's script; Intense contact
    after birth; presentation ceremony.

    Adoption service since 1983; Birthparent and couple
    may become friends; Counseling for adoptive
    parents; Three siblings, two families; Pati's story; Six
    couples interviewed; Adoptive couple backs out; She
    makes another choice; Melissa and Ray's experience.

    Why don't they release? Hard to plan realistically;
    The historical picture; Survey of teenage mothers;
    Pregnant teenagers face difficult decision; Veronica's
    advice for teenagers; Shauna's choice; Shauna's pain
    continues; Birthgrandmother's reaction; Travis brings
    joy to Eric and Breanne; Effect of open adoption.

Preface

People tend to have strong opinions about adoption. Some vehemently oppose the whole concept. They feel a child should be reared by her biological parent(s) if at all possible. "This is our baby. No way would we let anyone else take him" is a common feeling of parents everywhere.

A teenager, herself a parent at age 15, told me that if a couple can't conceive a child themselves, they weren't "meant" to be parents. This teenager is an adoptee who knows nothing about her birthparents. At this point, she feels quite negative toward her adoptive parents.

At the other extreme is the woman who, concerned about the number of babies born to teenagers, said, "Isn't there a movement to take their babies away from those 'children having children'?" I replied that I wasn't aware of such a movement, and that I would be quite concerned if such a thing happened.

"Well," she retorted, "How can these children possibly care for their babies? I'm an adoptive mother, and I know there are a lot of people out there who *want* those babies. Those children should not be allowed to keep them!"

Missing in both examples is a real concern for birthparents. Adoption needs to be an option for parents unable or not ready to become fulltime parents — including parents who want more for their child than they can provide. Adoption needs to be an option in which birthparents are a fully recognized and very important part of the adoption triangle.

For several generations, adoption agencies have routinely treated infant adoption as a "closed" process. Adoptive parents and birthparents have not been allowed to know each other's names or, for many years, anything at all about each other.

The birthparents were to forget about the baby, and the baby was to grow up as if he had been born into his adoptive family. Even his original birth certificate was sealed by the courts, and a new one issued listing only his adoptive parents with no mention of adoption or of his biological heritage.

Adoptees searching for their birthparents and birthparents attempting to find their birthchildren caused society to recognize the problems inherent in the closed, secret system.

Today, more and more licensed adoption agencies across the country are providing some degree of openness between birthparents and adoptive parents. Some are encouraging meetings and continued contact after the adoption is finalized. Independent adoption services are providing the same kind of openness, and some are offering the counseling which has been an important part of agency services.

"In open adoption, out goes the secrecy, and in comes the trust," an adoption professional observed. Truly, open adoption appears to be the form of adoption which best meets the needs of everybody in the adoption triangle.

October, 1986

Foreword

Teenage pregnancy continues to be one of the most critical societal issues confronting the nation. The 1.1 million teenage pregnancies reported by The Alan Guttmacher Institute in 1978 increased by 10,000 the following year and dropped back to the 1978 total in 1981. During the same period, the teenage pregnancy rate increased while the vulnerable population of teenagers declined by 300,000. Although 433,000 of the 1981 teenage pregnancies were terminated by abortion and 149,000 ended in miscarriages, there were 527,000 live teenage births. Adoption was the plan for only four percent of these children.

Almost every index of disturbance or pathology, including low birth weight, infant mortality, physical disabilities and retardation, can be positively related to being born to a teenage mother. The chances of the baby being physically abused and of later becoming delinquent or drug addicted are far greater if the baby is born to a teenage mother rather than to a woman in her twenties.

The stunted world of teen parents is grim. Their chances of completing a high school education, obtaining a good job, or marrying someone who will still be in the picture a few years hence are minimal. Most of the babies born to teen parents each year end up on the welfare rolls.

Society's answer to this problem must include a broadening of the options available to the pregnant teenager who becomes an adolescent mother before she is ready or able to be a nurturing parent. She needs to know and understand that adoption can be a responsible parenting plan, and that she and the baby's father can participate in the selection of the adopting parents. They can meet with them if they choose, direct hospital placement can be arranged, and regular updates on the child's progress can be received.

Open adoption offers all of these opportunities to birthparents. In the following book, Jeanne Lindsay discusses the availability of open adoption through independent channels, including attorneys and adoption services, as well as through licensed adoption agencies. My bias on the side of licensed adoption agencies comes from knowing and working with adoption social workers over three decades, having served first as a consultant and then as the state director of public affairs and public education for Children's Home Society of California. CHS has placed more than 42,000 children for adoption, more than any other agency. I base my preference for licensed adoption agency service on the fact that the agency will always be there. Adoption is a lifelong process which has to be integrated in different ways at different points in the lives of birthparents, adoptees, and adoptive parents. The licensed adoption agency can be a resource for the individuals involved in adoption throughout their lives; the absence of post-legal adoption services in independent or private adoption services warrents continuing concern.

Although not a social worker, I began advocating for more openness in adoption in 1974 as a result of interviewing 152 unmarried teenage mothers who were raising their children as single mothers. The in-depth interviews were done during the research phase of Children's Home Society's documentary film, "Growing Up Together: Four Teen Mothers and Their Babies." Thirty-seven of the 152 mothers with whom I spent at least one hour were then interviewed on camera, and we eventually selected the four best situations to film for the documentary. In answer to the question, "Did you ever consider adoption for your child?" two young mothers reported talking with an agency and one had discussed adoption with an attorney. The responses to "Why didn't you consider adoption?" were 149 variations of "Because I couldn't stand never knowing what happened to my baby."

Teachers and other professionals working with pregnant teens tell us that only the strongest, most self-sufficient young women are able to plan adoption today. Social workers at Children's Home Society told me that it was generally the most mature birthmother with a good self-image and plans for her own future development who was able to implement an adoption plan. The criticism and scorn heaped on relinquishing teenagers by their peers and their families can be withstood only by those young women strong enough to cope with the lack of supporting reassurance and acceptance of their adoption decision. When a birthmother not yet ready or able to be a parent decides to give the child nurturing parents who will provide what the child needs, that decision needs to be supported and approved.

While doing research for Children's Home Society's 1976 magazine entitled "The Changing Face of Adoption", which explored attitudes with respect to sealed adoption records, I talked with many birthparents who had relinquished or surrendered children, with adult adoptees, and with adoptive parents about their feelings regarding adoption and the secrecy that surrounded it. Then, a year later, it was my privilege to write the "Report of Research: The Changing Face of Adoption," which summarized the findings from 1,891 questionnaires returned from birthparents, adoptees, adoptive parents, and others. What insight this gave me into the pain that is experienced by all three parties in the adoption triad! Birthparents who plan adoption never forget, and never lose their concern and love for the child they have borne. Adoptees seldom search for a mother or a father; they search for the genetic connection that links them to what has gone before and what will come in the future. Adoptive parents cry deep inside because this much-loved son or daughter is not their own flesh. We understand now that adoption is not "the same as though born there," but it is a way of building families. It can also be the best plan for certain birthparents, for the children they have borne, and for the parents who adopt these children.

Young people, and their parents, need to learn more about adoption and to understand that it can often be the most loving and responsible decision that birthparents can make for their child. Until adoption is brought into the mainstream of society, however, we cannot successfully erase its image as a "throwaway" plan for a child. The only way to bring about more understanding of adoption is to open up the process and thereby increase acceptance of this way of creating families.

Open adoption offers a means of lessening the pain of the individuals involved. First of all, it empowers birthparents by giving them a say in the lives of their children. This is the birthparents' inherent right, and a right that is being denied them in adoption agencies that are not offering open adoption as an option. Healthy infants available for adoption are a very scarce commodity, yet, the numbers of couples unable to achieve biological parenthood are increasing. This means that birthparents are in the driver's seat and can dictate the kind of adoption they want for their children. If birthparents can be helped to understand the power that is theirs, they can require the kind of adoption they want. Birthparents have a right to know that open adoption can make them equal partners in an adoption plan that will give the child full opportunity for healthy development, while giving the birthparents the peace and satisfaction of knowing that they have fulfilled their parenting responsibilities. Open adoption has the added advantage of clarifying for the adopting parents the reality that their child has two sets of parents, and will have all of his or her life.

I do not believe, however, that open adoption is right for all birthparents or for all adoptive parents. It would be as much of a mistake to require that all adoptions be open as it was to make all of them secret. With the present degree of openness, there are childless couples who "go along" with what is expected (or required) in an open adoption without having the slightest intention of fulfilling an agreement which sets forth the extent of openness wanted and expected by the birthparents. While this is dishonesty and fraud on the part of the adoptive parents, it has happened and birthparents have had no recourse. The best safeguard that birthparents have to avoid this happening is to use the services of a reputable licensed adoption agency. The family study of prospective adoptive parents that is done by an accredited, licensed adoption agency offers the best protection for the birthparents, the child, and the adopting parents. One of the objectives in the counseling of both birthparents and adoptive parents by the adoption social worker in a licensed agency would be the determination of readiness for openness in the adoption.

I'm happy to see Jeanne Lindsay's book expand the information available to the individuals for whom adoption should be an option, particularly young teenage women. For their sakes, I hope her evaluation of the adoption services she has featured in this volume is objective, and that they continue to provide the level of service she describes. I believe that young people, and their parents, will gain new understanding of adoption from the individual stories Ms. Lindsay has chronicled. Most of all, I hope that young expectant parents not yet able or willing to provide the nurturing a child must have will be inspired by this book to evaluate adoption as an option open to them.

Charlotte De Armond
Communications Consultant

Acknowledgments

A great many people contributed to this book. I especially appreciate the 66 individuals, at least 45 personally involved in an adoption triangle, who granted me formal interviews. A few prefer not to be mentioned on this page. The others, while requesting anonymity in their stories, gave me permission to thank them publicly.

They include Kelly Bridges Lewis, Tammy Layton, Barbara Kugler, Sandy and Ric Woodhall, Regina Wisler, Jeff and Peggy McLain, Wendy Parker, Glen and Cherie Sawyer, Julie Thomas, Marion Summers, Katherine Goldy, Judy Albrecht, Wendy Matuz, Kim Cosenza, Kathy Johnstone, Julie Ackerman, Jodie Flory, Vickie and Chuck Potter, Deborah Kroeger, Tracy McCulley, Ken and B.J. Sorenson, Lillian Earnest Gonzalez, and Victorie McEvoy.

Extremely helpful were staff members of the adoption agencies and independent adoption services featured in this book. They include Helen Magee, Linda Brunner, Claire Priester, Karyn Johnson, Janet Cravens-Garner, Kathleen Silber, Pat Dornan, Bruce Rappaport, Sally Watson, Jeanne Etter, Sue Monarch, Jackie Radus, Louise Guinn, and Julia L. Richardson.

For years, I have considered Charlotte De Armond, long with Children's Home Society of California, *the* expert on adoption matters. She was a tremendous help several years ago when I was writing *Pregnant Too Soon: Adoption Is an Option*. I am especially pleased that she agreed to write the Foreword to *Open Adoption: A Caring Option*.

Others who shared information and provided guidance on the topic of open adoption include Linda Nunez, Sharon Kaplan, Reuben Pannor, Sister Maureen Joyce, Carolyn Fowler, Linda West, Bill Pierce, Debbie Giguere, and Catherine Monserrot.

Mary, Toby, Breanne and Keegan Crowley and Cary, Sharon,and Jessica Tice agreed to pose for Joyce Young of Buckner and Young Photography. Other photographs were provided by Glen and Cherie Sawyer, Helen Magee, and others who prefer to be anonymous.

Anne DeWitt designed the book's cover and provided guidance on book design. Bette Marcoe, 1st Impression Typesetting, completed the typesetting within the impossible period of time I requested. Delta Lithograph printed the book.

Julie Vetica and Sr. Maureen Joyce provided excellent editing assistance. Carole Blum deserves special thanks for taking care of everything else so *Open Adoption* could be written.

Bob, of course, deserves the most thanks of all. For a man to start marriage in the fifties with a wife completely in charge of day-to-day home affairs, then move in the eighties — with the same wife — to being in charge himself — at least during book-writing time — of the laundry, the bills, the shopping, sometimes the cooking, takes a very special man. He is, and I love him.

Introduction

In my work with pregnant and parenting teenagers, I have observed 15-year-olds who have become good mothers. I have also seen many teenagers not ready to parent who felt they must choose between abortion and single parenthood, or for some, too-early marriage. The young women with whom I work choose to be parents in the sense they do not opt for abortion.

The other choice — adoption — is rarely considered. Often I have heard young women who, even though they believe abortion is wrong, insist that adoption is even worse. Their vision of adoption is that of a mother who doesn't care about her baby, and who gives that baby away. There are no loving adoptive parents in that vision simply because, in traditional adoption, the birthparents never saw, met, or even knew who the adoptive parents were.

Who would hire a babysitter even for an hour without meeting and knowing something about that person? Yet this is exactly what a birthparent is expected to do in traditional adoption. My students know you don't leave a baby alone with a stranger. To them, adoption is not only leaving one's baby with a stranger, it is *giving* that baby to the stranger — forever. They are not interested. Neither are their parents or their peers.

Open Adoption Offers Choices

Birthparents who make an *open* adoption plan for their child have choices. First, they may choose the adoptive parents from descriptions and photos. They may meet them. They may even interview several before they make their decision... just as responsible parents do before choosing a babysitter. Both birthparents may stay in contact with their child.

Choosing adoptive parents is a far more serious decision than selecting an appropriate babysitter for this child they love dearly. The adoptive parents they select will be their child's parenting parents, and they know that choosing the right couple may well be the most important decision they ever make.

Several years ago a student of mine decided, when her daughter was five months old, that she could no longer parent. She saw a county adoption counselor once. In that session she asked, "If I give Maria up for adoption, will I ever see her again?" The counselor replied, "No, not after you sign the relinquishment papers."

The young mother could not face the prospect of totally losing contact with Maria. She sent her back to live with a recently-divorced aunt who already had three pre-school children and was relying on welfare for financial support. She may be a wonderful parent for Maria. However, I would have liked to offer Maria's mother a choice other than the closed adoption available at that time.

Today, pregnant teenagers and other pregnant women not ready to be parents may find in open adoption a choice which they can accept. To be able to stay in contact with her child is a significant change from handing her baby over to a social worker and knowing she will never see her child again.

Today's parents-too-soon and parents-at-the-wrong-time can choose open adoption. In some areas of the United States, licensed adoption agencies and independent adoption services provide this option. This book offers a look at this new world of adoption.

Not only are some of these agencies and services described, but most important, each chapter contains an account of the personal experiences of adoptive parents and birthparents who share their reasons for choosing this kind of adoption. Both the adoptive parents and the birthparents often mention the value for the child in this arrangement. It allows the child to know she has two sets of parents who love her, the "real" Mom and Dad with whom she lives, and the birthparents who loved her enough to choose a better life for her than they could provide at the time of her birth.

Interviews Provide Data

Interviewing professionals who work in the field of adoption has been exciting because adoption is changing so rapidly. I was fascinated with the missionary zeal of some of these professionals. Several of the agencies and independent adoption services proudly stress their uniqueness. "We're the only agency offering mediation in adoption." "We were the first to provide face-to-face meetings." "We are the only ones who..."

Occasionally one of these people would also warn me about another group that has "gone too far." Then I would visit the group "going too far" and find that they, too, were excited about helping birthparents and adoptive parents plan together for the best possible adoption for themselves and for their child.

Sometimes, in their enthusiasm for openness in adoption, individuals criticized licensed adoption agencies as being determined to stay in charge of adoption planning, and, in so doing, ignoring to a large extent the needs of the birthparents and the adoptive parents.

Several of the birthparents I interviewed mentioned going first to an agency where the caseworker seemed cold and uncaring. I report these comments only to remind us all of the tender loving care needed by all parties in the adoption triangle. Caseworkers are human beings who have occasional bad days, and who may experience burnout.

This is not meant to excuse insensitivity on anyone's part. However, I know many caring, empathetic adoption professionals in, as well as outside of, licensed adoption agencies. This book in no way is meant to be anti-agency. My goal is to discuss the beautiful things happening in the area of openness in adoption in some adoption agencies and in some independent/private adoption services.

The most exciting part of the interviewing was talking with birthparents and adoptive parents. Their enthusiasm for open adoption, their trust and caring concern for each other, and above all, their love for their babies were inspiring.

After listening to all of these people discuss openness in adoption from a professional and/or personal standpoint, I have formed my own opinion of the extent of openness, *coupled with counseling,* which I consider advisable. I believe that full openness means the birthparents and adoptive parents not only meet, but also exchange fully identifying information.

I believe this complete openness should be available to all parties in the adoption triangle. The key, to me, is the preferences of the birthparents and the adoptive parents involved. One agency director claimed to offer open adoption, yet stated that, to date, no adoptive parents/birthparents have exchanged identifying information. Somehow I doubt that their clients truly understand that this kind of adoption is available to them.

If their clients do not wish to share their full names and addresses with each other, I understand the need for the agency acting as a go-between. A few of the people I interviewed mentioned that letters between adoptive parents and birthparents were read by the agency caseworker to ensure that no identifying information was exchanged. That bothered me. If I want to give my address to someone, that's my business. Adoptive and birthparents should have the same option with no questions asked.

In most of the agencies and adoption services described in this book, this doesn't appear to be a problem. Exchange of identifying information is the prerogative of the parties involved. I believe this is the way it should be.

Legal Aspects of Adoption

If you are involved in any way with adoption, personally or professionally, know the laws in your state or, in Canada, in your province. If you don't like those laws, you can work toward changing them, but first, you need to know and understand current laws. Is independent/private adoption legal in your area? In a few states, it is not. Because laws concerning adoption are changing rapidly, no attempt is made in this book to cover this important topic.

Laws pertaining to adoption vary a great deal from one state to another. Generally, to finalize the adoption, the birthfather's signature is required as well as the birthmother's.

In some placements, both birthparents are deeply involved in planning for their child's future. Other birthmothers are alone as they work out their adoption plans. For simplicity in this book, the singular form, birthparent, is often used. It is important to remember that the birthfather has equal rights with the mother in adoption planning. Ideally, he is also deeply involved in the counseling.

One birthfather's story is included in *Open Adoption*, and I would have liked to include many accounts of birthfathers' experiences. Many of the birthmothers quoted, however, explain that they were no longer with their babies' fathers when they made the adoption decision. Some of these birthfathers were involved in the adoption planning, but were not available for interviewing.

The masculine pronoun is more often used in referring to the baby in the following chapters, not because most adopted children are boys, but to differentiate easily from the feminine pronouns referring to the birthmothers.

High Cost of Adoption

Adopting a baby is expensive. Placement fees of the agencies described in the following chapters are as high as $7,400. Generally, this fee covers legal costs, counseling, and other expenses of the placement. Independent adoption may cost more. It is not legal or ethical to buy a baby. It is legal to pay "necessary expenses related to pregnancy" which may mean not only medical expenses but also living expenses for the birthmother. Legal services, so necessary in an adoption, are expensive.

In addition to paying these costs, the adoptive couple utilizing an independent adoption service must pay for that service. People need to be paid a fair fee for their services. What constitutes a fair fee is the dilemma.

There are two obvious problems in the high cost of adoption. First, some couples who would be wonderful parents cannot afford these costs. Couples in this situation should check with local adoption agencies to see if there is a sliding fee scale based on income. This arrangement sometimes makes adoption possible for low-income people. Sometimes the placement fee is waived and continuing financial help is available for families wishing to adopt special needs children.

The other major problem is the risk of paying "too much" for an adoption. As I interviewed the professionals, the birthparents, and the adoptive parents for this book, I heard rumors of adoption services charging thousands of dollars for a baby. At what point does this turn into baby-buying? Where does one draw the line?

Linda Nunez, Tustin, California, is an attorney who handles independent adoption cases. Unlike many attorneys specializing in adoption, Nunez insists on counseling for the birthparents. She also provides reading assignments about open adoption for both birthparents and adoptive parents. She feels that adoption services and attorneys sometimes "get greedy" and charge too much for their services.

"You should insist on the fees being set in the beginning," she stressed. "If you are paying medical expenses, those can spiral if, for example, the birthmother needs a C-section. But you should know what the attorney is charging, the costs involved in going through an adoption service, and the expectations of the birthmother concerning possible living expenses. If you find costs rising higher and higher, you probably should pull back," she cautioned.

Difficulties of Choosing

This book is packed with success stories of birthparents who feel they have found good parents for the child they don't feel they can parent, and of adoptive parents who finally have the child they have wanted for so long. These stories are all true. Only the names and a few details have been changed to protect the anonymity of these people.

However, each time an adoptive couple is chosen to parent someone's baby, other would-be adoptive couples are not chosen. The heartbreak continues of not having the child they long for. Whether the birthparents or the agencies do the choosing, the selection process means some applicants are left out. Either way, it's a difficult situation for the couple who does not get the baby.

A couple who may be very successful professionally and socially may find it hard to be interviewed by a very young birthmother or by birthparents who, for whatever reason, feel they cannot parent their child. The adoptive father in chapter 10 said that sometimes he tries to put himself in that young birthmother's place. In this way, he gains a deeper understanding of her situation.

Several adoptive parents mentioned how frightened they were of the idea of open adoption *until* they met birthparents for the first time, usually in a counseling setting.

They learn how much birthparents care about their children, how much they love them. They realize that for some parents not yet ready to play the parenting role, making and carrying out an adoption plan for their child shows tremendous love and caring.

Finding the right parents for their child is hard for birthparents. Going through the process of attempting to be chosen is hard for the adoptive parents. A great deal of trust and caring is needed on both sides.

Adoption encompasses far more than non-relative, in-country, infant adoption. Step-parent adoption happens often in our society. Couples are adopting infants from other countries. Many older children including children with special needs have been freed for adoption. Finding permanent homes for these children is an important challenge.

Open Adoption: A Caring Option, however, is a discussion of the placing of United States-born infants with adoptive couples to whom they are not related, and of the birthparents of these infants.

More than 1,100,000 teenagers become pregnant in the United States each year. Only 4 percent of those who deliver a child make an adoption plan for that child.

I think open adoption will change those adoption statistics. More important, open adoption offers a caring, loving approach for all people involved in the adoption triangle.

1

The Changing
Adoption Drama

The birth of a baby is a dramatic event. Adoption is a dramatic event. Combine the two and you have a real cliffhanger. Characters include, in order of appearance, birthmother and birthfather (although he may stay offstage), the baby, and the adoptive parents.

Basic plot: Two people who feel they can't or would rather not parent a child at this time make an adoption plan for their baby.

Act 1. Two people who want children try for years to get pregnant but it doesn't happen. They undergo extensive infertility testing and finally face the reality of being different, of not being able to conceive. (Couples who have endured — and survived — the infertility rites of modern medicine do well, as one adoptive parent expressed it, to maintain a sense of humor.) The couple may feel their dreams of having a family are gone, thrown out with the final infertility test.

Act 2. The pregnancy — someone else's. Every pregnancy, planned or unplanned, wanted or not, is a drama in the lives of the participants. Each birthparent has a different story from all the rest, but when she/they decide to make an adoption plan, the drama intensifies.

Act 3. The birth. The birthparents carry out their adoption plan. The adoptive parents have their eagerly-awaited child.

Three Different Scripts

A simple script — but this play can be staged in three very different ways. First, the traditional drama, the way adoption has been acknowledged during much of this century, a script created by many adoption workers and adoptive parents:

Act 1. The couple goes through the infertility testing, but they don't tell their friends. They decide to adopt a baby and pretend it is their biological child.

Act 2. For this one, the birthfather doesn't exist. The birthmother may have been a nice girl but she has sinned and does not deserve to have this baby. Her obvious solution is to place it for adoption so she can go on with her life as if the pregnancy never happened. She is not involved in the adoption planning, and she never sees her baby.

Act 3. The baby is born. S/he stays in a foster home briefly until the birthparents sign relinquishment papers. Then the adoptive parents pick up their baby. They have no contact with the birthparents. For them, the baby's biological parents are shrouded in secrecy and they intend to keep it that way. They act as if this baby was born to them.

Act 4. The happy, well-adjusted adoptee never wonders about his birthparents, and they forget that he ever existed.

The true-to-life story of many traditional adoptions is *not* the fantasy enacted above. The second version of this drama more accurately portrays reality:

Act 1. The infertility tests don't change, and the couple grieves over the child they will never conceive. They proceed with adoption plans.

Act 2. The pregnancy remains a drama, and the birthfather may or may not be on stage with the birthmother. They decide on an adoption plan which means she/they will lose their baby just as surely as if that baby died.

Because they have never met and know very little about
the adoptive parents, their grief is intensified. They don't
have the finality of death. There is no grave, and the
grieving may have no end. As birthparents, they are
expected to hide the fact that they have a child somewhere,
which means the adoption plan must have been a
shameful act. Guilt is added to the grief.

Act 3. The infertile couple adopts the child. They know
nothing about the birthparents, but figure they must have
not loved this child since they gave him away.
Nevertheless, they panic at the thought of the
birthmother's reappearance. What if she finds them? She
would certainly take her child back! Even when he's
grown, they fear his birthmother. Surely she could destroy
their happy family.

Act 4. The baby grows up. Early in life he feels he is
different. He figures if his birthparents gave him away,
they must not have loved him — and if Mother and Dad
won't even talk about those birthparents, they must have
been terrible people indeed. Somehow he feels something
is missing, and begins to wonder more and more about the
possibility of meeting his birthparents.

He may search for them although he knows his adoptive
parents would be horrified if he made contact with them.
When he starts to search, he finds he doesn't have access
to his own birth records. He knows he can see his school
records and his employment files, but his biological
identity is denied to him. He begins to search, and learns
that to do so he must utilize techniques Sherlock Holmes
himself would admire.

These two dramas have been played over and over
through closed adoption practices of both agency and
independent adoption throughout the last two or three
generations. But there can be a different drama, a drama
even more exciting, less threatening, and far more
satisfying to all characters:

Act 1. Infertility testing is still a hassle. But the couple
may be able to realize this is the handicap they must

accept. They grieve, hopefully briefly, for their lost biological child(ren), then get on with their lives.

They contact either a licensed agency or a good independent/private adoption service and say they want to adopt a baby. They go to seminars, meet other would-be adoptive parents and, most important, birthparents. They learn that birthparents are real people who care about their babies and who want good homes for them. They discover these birthparents are not at all frightening.

Act 2. The difficulties of the unplanned pregnancy may not change. But when she/they decide to make an adoption plan, they have choices, most important of which may be the chance to choose the adoptive parents, meet them, and perhaps have an on-going relationship with them.

Act 3. The birthparents choose the couple to adopt their baby. They meet, and both couples (or the birthmother and the adoptive parents) discuss their hopes and dreams for this baby. They talk about exchanging pictures and letters, and about meeting occasionally through the years ahead.

The baby is born. The birthparents hold him, feed him, love him. Three days later they present him to the adoptive parents — they know this is the greatest gift they will ever give anyone. They are grieving, and the adoptive parents are torn between the grief they know the birthparents are experiencing and the joy they feel as they take their baby home.

Act 4. The baby grows up knowing he has two sets of parents who love him. His adoptive parents are his "real" parents, the people who care for him daily and who he can always count on for support. But in addition, he has birthparents he sees occasionally who also love him. He knows his roots, he won't ever have to go to court to plead with a judge to open his records, and he is able to get on with his life.

Defining Open Adoption

Open adoption — is it the rainbow at the end of the adoption tunnel — or is it as risky as a hailstorm on a freshly sprouted garden?

First of all, what is open adoption? The definition varies. A cautious social worker may feel she is practicing open adoption because she encourages her birthmother clients to write a letter to their babies — with no identifying information whatsoever. She has discovered that the letter helps the birthmother deal with her grief. It may mean a great deal to the child who otherwise might assume his mother "gave him away" because she didn't care. ("Making an adoption plan" is a more accurate description of this process than is "giving him away.")

At the other end of the spectrum are the advocates of cooperative adoption. Sharon Kaplan, co-author of *Cooperative Adoption: A Handbook* (1984: Triadoption Publications), and director of Parenting Resources in Tustin, California, describes cooperative adoption as the child's access to both families, to both sets of parents.

She writes, "If the child has access to both families, (s)he does not lose anything, and both sets of parents, by the nature of the arrangement will have continued access to each other." (page 1) She feels the best adoption practice means keeping the birthparents as fully involved as possible with the adoptive parents in rearing their child...but it does *not* mean co-parenting, she hastens to add. "Successful cooperative adoption implies that the adoptive parents are in charge," she stressed.

For this book, open adoption means the birthparents and the adoptive parents meet and have the opportunity to have an on-going relationship with each other if either party wishes to do so. The adoptive parents are the "real" parents because they are responsible for the child in the practical day to day, year by year sense. The birthparents may visit a few times during the child's early years, or they may maintain a relationship throughout their lives.

The adoptee in a truly open adoption knows this other woman is his "birthmother," and he may be in contact with his birthfather. At the same time, he knows his real parents are Mom and Dad. "So what's the big deal?" he may ask.

It is a big deal, however, to many people in the United States where adoption for several generations has been closed — closed, at least, as far as nearly all adoption agencies were concerned. For many years, adoption agencies were bound by law — and still are in some states — to prevent contact between birthparents and their baby's adoptive parents.

The baby's original birth certificate was — and still is — replaced with a new document listing the adoptive parents as the mother and father. This birth certificate contains no mention of adoption or the identity of the birthparents. The original certificate is sealed, and in most states, cannot be opened without a court order.

Reasons For Closed Adoption

This was/is done to protect the privacy of both the birthparents and the adoptive couple. It was also assumed that this was in the best interests of the child. However, the many adult adoptees searching for their birthparents today deny this assumption. Many birthparents, too, have come out of the closet in recent years and have insisted that the closed adoption was not of their choosing.

Independent adoption, legal in most states, has often meant open adoption inasmuch as the name of the birthparents and the adoptive parents are included on the adoption papers. In California, for example, independent adoption by law means the birthparents place their baby directly with the adopting couple. In practice, however, independent adoption of non-related infants is likely to be carried out through a doctor or a lawyer with the adoptive parents never meeting the birthparents.

Independent adoption is considered high-risk by many adoption professionals because of the lack of counseling. The adoption drama tends to be a harsh one. The pain caused by giving away one's child seems obvious. The pain endured by couples who desperately want to conceive a child but do not succeed is also real. Simply handing a baby from one set of parents to another doesn't solve everyone's problems. If professional counseling is ever needed for life crises, surely it is needed here.

Agency Versus Independent Adoption

Professional counseling has been an important factor with agencies. A good agency is expected to provide counseling services for its birthparent clients, preferably counseling service which extends past the placement of the baby. In fact, a birthmother may need more help from her counselor after placement than she did before.

The agency, through its home studies and follow-up contacts with adoptive families, also provides counseling for these couples. It is important that adoptive couples deal with the hurt of their infertility, that they become accepting of it, *before* they adopt a child. A good agency assists in this process through counseling.

For many years, the choice for birthparents considering an adoption plan for their baby was either independent adoption without counseling or private agency adoption. Adoptive parents had the same choice. Each could go to an agency and expect to receive counseling. People generally felt working with an agency was less risky than independent adoption.

For one thing, the birthparents relinquished their baby directly to the agency. The baby was then legally free before the adoptive parents took over his care. Birthparents were expected to think this was less risky for them, too. If the baby was born with a problem, the agency would take the responsibility of dealing with the handicap. If the birthparents planned to release independently, perhaps the adoptive parents would back out of the agreement at this point.

One big advantage of independent/private adoption was that the baby was placed with the adoptive family immediately. He went from the hospital directly to his new parents. Bonding could begin at once. During the last decade, however, many agencies have been speeding up placement. Sometimes the baby relinquished to an agency is able to go directly from the hospital to her permanent home.

Another possible advantage of independent placement was that birthparents could, if they insisted, have more control over the adoption plan. They could meet the parents, could even plan an open adoption with continuing contact. This was not generally done however. Independent adoptions of non-related infants, as mentioned above, have tended for some time to be closed with no real contact between the birthparents and adoptive parents.

I have worked with pregnant teenagers since 1972. My dilemma, when a student was considering an adoption plan, was whether to encourage independent adoption or advise her to contact a licensed adoption agency. I was pro-agency for many years because I thought it was extremely important that my students have good counseling.

I knew our local agencies were not "baby-stealers" as teenagers occasionally labeled them. The caseworkers wanted to help each individual make the best decision for herself and her baby. Caseworkers explained that if a girl had doubts about the wisdom of placing her baby for adoption, they didn't want her to follow through with her adoption plan. Whenever possible, they offered the same type of counseling to the birthfather.

At the same time I was advocating agency adoption, I was concerned that the birthparent was the forgotten point of the adoption triangle, the parent always in the shadows. I knew from observing these young women that they did not simply release their babies, then go back to life as it was. They could never go back.

Perhaps, I thought, if she went through independent adoption, she could know more about her child's placement. Would this help lessen the pain of losing that child? But I would always remind myself of the riskiness and the lack of counseling in independent adoption.

Trying a Different Way

Then two or three years ago I met a woman who had placed her child for adoption 22 years earlier. It was a closed adoption and she knew nothing of her child's family or of his life. She experienced a great deal of pain through the years as she wondered about her lost child. She decided there must be a better way, so, after some research and lots of serious thinking, she and a friend opened an adoption service.

An important part of that service (not an agency) was the provision of counseling for the birthparents and the adoptive parents. Another crucial element was the openness of the adoptions. Adoptive parents provided descriptions and pictures of themselves, their homes, and their families. Birthparents read these profiles, then chose their child's adoptive parents.

This choice generally involved meeting and actually interviewing the adoptive parents. Sometimes there would be several meetings before delivery. Perhaps the adoptive parents took the birthmother to her doctor's appointments. They might be with her in the hospital when she delivered.

This was a wild new concept for me, and it seemed a bit radical. Then, as an anthropologist, I started thinking of other cultures in the world where adoption is a simple process of handing a child from one set of parents to another. Sometimes the birthparents can't or don't want to parent this child. Other times the adoptive parents want a child and the birthparents decide to oblige them by giving them a baby. But it's not a shameful thing. The adoption doesn't have to be hidden.

Was it possible to make this process work in our culture?
I started talking with adoption agency people who were slowly shifting from absolute secrecy to more and more openness in their adoption placements. Describing several adoptive couples to the birthparent and letting her choose the couple who would receive her child became

commonplace. So did encouraging the birthmother to write a letter to her baby to explain why she was placing him for adoption.

Gradually a few agencies across the country changed their policies. It's becoming more and more common for the adoptive parents to agree to send pictures of the baby to the birthparent, perhaps to write her a letter of appreciation. This can satisfy some of the birthparent's concern about the health and wellbeing of her child.

These contacts may be carried out through the agency, with no identifying information released. In some agencies, the birthparents and the adoptive parents meet after placement, and in a few, before actual relinquishment of the baby. Sometimes they exchange identifying information and continue to stay in contact with each other.

The exciting aspect of these developments is that some adoption agencies are offering some of the openness formerly available through independent adoption. At the same time, some independent adoption services are offering counseling formerly available primarily through agencies. Each is taking good aspects from the other and incorporating these changes into their own day to day actions.

Adoption Is Changing

The point is that adoption is changing. More and more efforts are being directed toward making adoption as sensitive as possible to the needs of all three parts of the triangle — the birthparents, the adoptive parents, and the adoptee.

Some of the following chapters contain descriptions of agencies and independent adoption services which provide the opportunity for birthparents and adoptive parents to meet and to discuss their hopes and their dreams for this child who is so important to each of them. These parents, birth and adoptive, can also discuss the degree and amount of contact they want with one another in the future.

There is no chapter devoted to positive aspects of the birthparents simply placing their child through their doctor or attorney. It is the rare birthparent who can cope well with an adoption plan which does not include good counseling. Open adoption is a wonderful idea, but one that relies on a great deal of trust and sensitivity on the part of all persons involved.

As one counselor put it, "Trust is supremely important, but trust can be helped along through education." Education is a basic part of adoption counseling. If adoptive parents understand the pain of the birthmother as she loses her baby, and if the birthparent understands the needs of the adoptive couple, their trust for each other is likely to be greater.

Reuben Pannor, former Director of Community Services, Vista Del Mar, West Los Angeles, California, is recognized as a leader in the field of open adoption. He defines open adoption as a process whereby, with counseling as needed, birthparents place their child with an adoptive couple of their choice, a couple to whom they relinquish legal, moral, and nurturing rights to the child. Birthparents retain the right to continuing contact with and to knowledge of the child's whereabouts and welfare. This kind of open adoption is what this book is all about.

Sonia's Story

Although Sonia still has not had a face to face meeting with her child's adoptive parents, she is in close touch with them. She receives letters and pictures from the adoptive parents regularly, and she knows that an actual meeting is possible if she wishes.

A vivacious and attractive brunette, Sonia was a junior in high school the winter her child was born. Hers was a high school romance which ended abruptly midway through her pregnancy.

She transferred to a special school for pregnant and parenting teenagers, a school where the overwhelming majority of students keep their babies to rear themselves. Nine months after Angela Karen was born, Sonia shared her story:

My family took it great. They left it up to me whether I would keep the baby or release. I found out after I released her that my mom thought about adopting her, but she figured it would confuse the baby. She thought I would come in on the weekends and want to have her.

At first I was going to keep her. My mom had a three-year-old and I had the crib in the garage and my baby clothes. But then I started wondering how I could support her. Babies get sick — how could I pay for that? I couldn't put that burden on my family.

My school counselor gave me the agency's phone number. I told my caseworker what I wanted in a family and she gave me descriptions of five families. I picked the one I wanted. Colette is a teacher and Chris is an engineer. I know their likes, I know their dislikes.

Colette had an unhappy childhood. I learned about that because I sent Karen the ring Jim (her birthfather) had given me. Colette sent me a letter in which she said she didn't know her father until late in life and never had a good relationship with him. She hopes this ring will mean as much to Karen as it does to her.

Colette and Chris had a daughter who lived 45 minutes. Colette said she could feel with me the pain of going home from the hospital without a baby.

I wrote one letter to them while I was pregnant, and I'm writing to them once a month now. My first letter was very emotional, but now it's everyday — what I'm doing in school and at work, and it's the same with them.

Colette and Chris know I'm getting married. They even know who I am. I did a video for the agency and they saw it. They were excited when they learned I was the one in the video. They were willing to name the baby Karen as I did, but I told them she's your child and you have the fun of naming her. So they made Karen her middle name — Angela Karen. I like it, but I still think of her as Karen. I probably always will.

Colette even wrote to Cathi, my school counselor, before Karen was born. She didn't thank Cathi for getting me to release the baby. Instead, Colette thanked her for being with me since she and Chris couldn't be here. I thought that was really neat. It shows how much they cared.

They have assured me they still call me her mother. Do you have any idea how much comfort that gives me? When I came home from the hospital they sent me this glass etching with rosebuds on it and engraved, "No love is dearer than a mother's love and no mother is dearer than you are."

The agency always reads our letters and censors them to make sure we aren't exchanging identifying information. Basically it's not an open adoption even though there is contact. I know where they live because of the sticker on the gift. If I wanted to, I could find Karen. I could go over to the Methodist Church on a Wednesday night and pick her up. But I don't feel any need to do so. I released her to go to that family to live her life. I put her out of my life and I don't really want to confuse myself or her or her parents by going back into her life.

Unless girls have been pushed into making the adoption decision, they have their own reasons for doing so. They feel comfortable in it, so why should they go back on it? I'm sure everybody has thought about it. I don't feel I need to find her. I made my decision and I made it on her behalf. I was sound in my decision. I assume it would be the same with others.

Postscript

About eight months after the above interview, Sonia's caseworker decided, because of Sonia's maturity and because it was her adoptive parents' wish, to arrange a meeting. They had become close, and Sonia had sent them an invitation to her wedding. Sonia said she would meet them anywhere at any time.

The adoptive parents couldn't bring Angela Karen, according to the social worker, because, although the confidentiality laws had been weakened in that state recently, any contact still had to be between consenting adults. The meeting was to be at the social worker's home, and all parties appeared to be thrilled.

However, the night before the meeting, to her surprise the social worker received a call from Sonia. She said she had changed her mind. She was grateful for the opportunity and she wanted to continue some contact, but she wanted it reduced. She said having the opportunity to meet Chris and Colette had made all the difference in the world. Knowing it was her choice, she didn't need the meeting after all.

After the above incident, I interviewed Angela Karen's parents. Their delight in their lovely daughter and their love for Sonia, her birthmother, is obvious:

Chris And Colette's Experience

Colette: Angela is 18 months old now and we think she's gorgeous. No matter where I take that child, people stop me and tell me how beautiful she is.

Chris: A friend told me yesterday she's the Gerber baby. She looks exactly like that baby.

Colette: It's hard to realize we still haven't met Sonia face to face, and that we communicate only through Lillian (social worker). She chose us before delivery, and we wrote our first letter to her the night before we went over to get Angela.

Chris: Back when we first started writing her, it was kind of like adopting a child and adopting a teenager. She had written Angela a letter and another letter to us, somebody opening her heart to us.

Colette: One reason she chose us was because we had lost our baby. She said when she left the hospital to go home, she told her grandma I would know exactly how she felt because I had come home from the hospital with empty arms too.

Chris: How did we get into the openness? I think the biggest thing were the letters from Sonia to Angela. They were so moving that, in thinking about her, we wanted to say something to her. Right off the bat we were a part of her life.

Even now when we tell people about writing to Sonia and sending pictures, they look at us like we're crazy or something, yet the more we do the closer we feel — like we found a new friend.

A year ago a man in the office told me they were interested in adopting. He saw the kinds of things we were doing but said he didn't think they could be that open. But they adopted a little boy six months ago, and now they send rolls of pictures and write these long missives, a real turnaround. Our boss listens to us both, and just shakes his head.

We were real excited about meeting Sonia while our friends were saying, "Oh, you shouldn't do that." All these things were going through our minds about what would happen with our relationship after this. When she called, we were kind of shocked at first. Then we realized that it's because everything is so open that she had been able to come to that decision.

I think having the meeting scheduled helped her get on with her life. We're real proud of her and what she's doing. We told Lillian that these doors are always open to Sonia.

Colette: I wrote Lillian a letter Monday night telling her I miss writing to Sonia — it's something I've done every month for a year and a half, and now there is this emptiness. So just in case — when she said she had decided not to meet us, I wrote her another letter and told her we respect her decision, and all she needs to do if she ever wants to see us is to let Lillian know.

Chris: We think her decision may reflect on her relationship with Dave, and that's very important, building their relationship.

After talking with Colette and Chris, I called Sonia. She and Dave are married now. I wanted to hear her reasons for cancelling the scheduled meeting. She explained:

Basically, I decided not to go ahead with the meeting because I'm ready to get on with my life and not live in the past. I need to let go for my sake and for Dave's, but also because Chris, Colette, and Angela Karen are a family now. Dave and I will have our own family.

I think if I didn't have all the pictures and letters from Colette and Chris, I'd have a harder time letting go. Open adoption was right for me, and I know we'll keep in touch. They're a beautiful family.

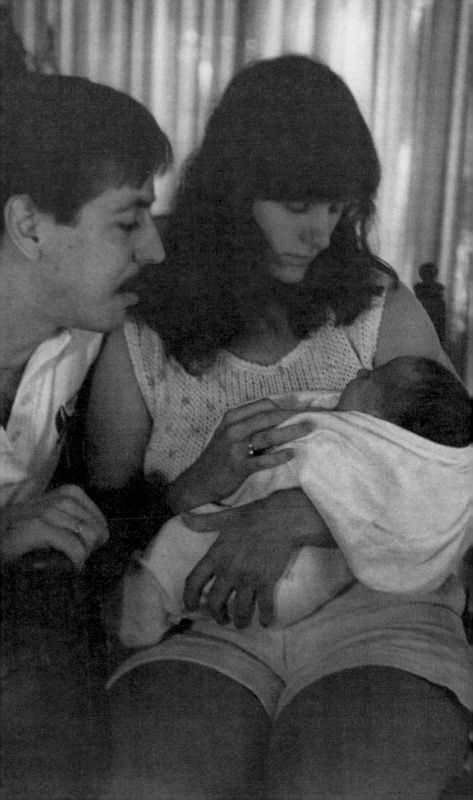

2

Options for Pregnancy —
Birthparents Come First

"Some of our clients who plan to release their infants for adoption take them home with them for a few days, even a couple of weeks. Then they say, "All right, now I've done some parenting and I've said my goodbyes. I'm ready to proceed — I know my plan of adoption was right," reported Helen West Magee, Director of Options for Pregnancy, the pregnancy counseling program of Adoption Services of WACAP, Seattle, Washington. Options is an example of a licensed adoption agency offering some openness in adoption.

Because they want to be absolutely sure their counseling staff remains totally involved in serving the needs of birthparents, Options was organized in 1978 as a separate part of WACAP (Western Association of Concerned Adoptive Parents). WACAP serves adoptive parents in Washington, Alaska, Idaho and Utah. Options assists birthparents throughout Washington State and is now offering services in Northern Utah and the major cities of Alaska.

"It is very clear in our agency that Options counselors advocate for the birthparents and adoption counselors advocate for the adoptive parents," Magee explained. "Birthmothers are our primary clients in Options."

Not All Clients Choose Adoption

The agency placed nearly 100 infants in 1985, and more than half that number during the first half of 1986. Yet slightly less than half of the birthmothers who remain with Options through delivery actually release for adoption.

"Of course families are terribly disappointed when they have been chosen and then the mother decides to parent her child. We do all we can to prepare them for that possibility. It helps when they have met the mother because they know her as a person," Magee stressed. "They have more empathy for her, and they can understand her feelings better than if she were unknown, just 'someone' out there keeping them from being parents."

Of their total clients, including those who contacted the agency only once or twice, those who miscarried, moved away, or simply disappeared, only 20 percent complete an adoption plan. Yet WACAP places more infants for adoption than many other agencies in the United States, according to Magee.

Options serves birthfathers and their families whenever possible, giving them support and choices as well. "We're here to help those involved in an unexpected pregnancy, whoever they are," Magee explained.

"We tailor-make our service to the client," she continued. "She is not made to fit into any preconceived pattern except as it pertains to law. We go to her and help her meet her own needs. We never urge or advise a client to release a child for adoption. It's her child, her life, her choice. But we do want her to make a cognitive choice, not drift into parenthood or adoption.

"In this country we hear so many women saying, 'Well, I'm pregnant. That means I have to have an abortion or I have to be a mother.' They do have another choice in adoption," Magee insists. "But, again, it is their lives and their children, and if they decide to be parents, let's help them do that. Let's find parenting classes for them, refer visiting nurses to them, help them be good, stable parents."

Options serves their parenting clients for two years following delivery, if they choose to remain with the program. But Magee sees a gradual return to adoption. "Women are often very relieved when they learn about open adoption. They prefer it to abortion or parenting before they're ready — but only when they can be actively involved in planning for their child's future, have information following placement, and be assured of confidentiality if they wish," she stated.

Openness Developed Over Time

Some form of open adoption has been practiced through Options since it was organized by a committee which included women who had experienced unplanned pregnancies and closed adoptions. In the first years of Options, birthparents, when they were about seven months pregnant, were allowed/encouraged to choose "their" adoptive parents from anonymous descriptions of WACAP adoptive parents.

Now adoptive parents write about themselves and illustrate with photos — photos of themselves, their home, their relatives, their pets. They are advised to include lots of pictures because these often say more to the birthparents than the written comments. Included in the presentation is a letter which gives a more personal touch to the description.

"We suggest they name their pets," Magee continued. "Either the birthparent had a pet that made her happy, or she wished she had one. One client chose a family because of their big dog - she had learned to walk by hanging on to a big dog. I told the family, and the father exclaimed, "Charlie gets steak tonight!"

After a birthmother has chosen her family, she starts corresponding with them. Generally they meet before delivery which lets the adoptive parents have some share in the pregnancy. "We, of course, honor the wishes of both - no birthparent is asked to do anything she doesn't want to do, nor are adoptive parents," Magee emphasized, then added, "But in most cases now they are meeting prior to birth."

All of these meetings include an Options counselor and often an adoption counselor as well as the birthparent(s) and the adoptive parents. The Options representative advocates for the birthparent(s) while the adoption counselor supports the adoptive parents.

Once they are comfortable, the birthparent(s) and adoptive parents usually spend some time alone together during the meeting, which may last three hours or more. Each meeting is unique, carefully planned, and guided by the counselors according to the needs and personalities of those involved.

"The chosen adoptive parents almost always develop a feeling of closeness to 'their' birthmother," Magee commented. "One adoptive mother said, 'I don't know how our birthmother is related to me. She isn't my niece or my cousin, sister or daughter, but somehow, some way, we have a relationship. There just isn't a name for it.'"

The agency still (in 1986) does not disclose last names, addresses, telephone numbers, place of employment, or even city of residence of adoptive or birthparents. But many of them, according to Magee, share those details on their own. "Sometimes they do so at placement and sometimes it's months later — with no encouragement from us," she emphasized. "We aren't practicing totally open adoption. We offer adoption with some openness in it." All correspondence goes through the Options office — until and unless the parties decide otherwise and share complete names and addresses.

Birthparents/Adoptive Parents Form Relationship

When the child is born, the adoptive mother frequently is the labor coach for the birthmother. Sometimes the adoptive father is also involved. Or the adoptive couple may not actually be in the delivery room, but is in the hospital. They can see the baby and take pictures immediately after delivery.

Being at the birth developed at the request of adoptive parents who said, "This is our only opportunity to see a birth, to be involved in it, to go to childbirth education classes. And," Magee muses, "when you think about it, how many adoptees ever get to hear their own birth stories?

"Then, after delivery, there must be some distance during the next few days so the birthmother can spend time with her child and so she won't feel forced into releasing the child. I'm a firm believer in our clients having lots of time and no pressure to make the final decision," Magee stressed.

As mentioned above, the birthmother may even take her baby home to parent for a night or a week or two before presenting him to the adoptive parents. Or, if she can't take the child home, she may place him in a WACAP receiving home where she can visit daily and bathe and feed the baby. It is her choice.

What happens to the adoptive parents during that time? The birthmother usually encourages them to visit the baby too, either alone or when she is present. This still allows her some time to make her final decision and the adoptive parents respect her right to do so.

The birthparent is usually with the adoptive parents again at placement. The agency is developing a placement ritual for this important milestone. "Presenting the child to the adoptive parents signifies a gift. It is not a wrenching or a pulling away of that child. It does not make our clients grieve any less, but somehow it serves as a needed rite of passage for the birthparents. The adoptive parents tell us that it helps them feel more entitled to be parents of the child," Magee commented.

And then, following placement, the correspondence continues with letters and pictures and occasionally a videotape of the baby at home with the adoptive parents. Near the first and/or second birthday, many birthparents and adoptive families meet again. Rather than upsetting birthparents, Options has found that it helps them close their acute grief. Communication continues by letter and perhaps telephone calls placed by counselors.

"It wasn't always like that in Options," Helen admits. "In the early years, a few families agreed to provide information or letters after placement, then were so fearful they refused to do so. Consequently, we have some clients who are still grieving severely. It makes me sad for the birthmothers and we do what we can for them — bits of information from time to time.

"It also saddens me for the adopted children when I think of the information they won't have about their birthfamilies, and the difficulty the adoptive parents are going to have answering the inevitable questions." Magee continued, "We were (still are) pioneers, and I guess it was bound to happen. Our birthmothers try to understand, but it is terribly hard on them. It all goes back to those myths that birthparents don't care about their children and that they forget—and that's a lot of rot!

"For the adoptive parents who genuinely accept the 'open' adoption philosophy, there really is hope of creating a family through adoption. For the birthparents, there is comfort, and for the adoptees there is information that helps them with their own identities. There is far less pain for everyone. We see birthmothers who seem to feel joy for the adoptive families even in the midst of their own pain."

Certainly the birthparents never forget, but seeing the child well and happy, developing normally, and closely bonded to the adoptive parents is very reassuring, according to the agency.

Counseling Is Crucial

Throughout the months of adoption planning, a lot of anticipatory grief counseling occurs. Options offers support groups for birthparents and support groups for their parents. "I maintain that two clients make a group.

Our girls grieve and they grieve hard. They often write journals and prepare gifts for their children. They talk with other women who have released children.

"We provide books for them to read and attorneys with whom they discuss their legal rights. We are gentle, but we don't gloss over how difficult completing an adoption plan will be. We never advise adoption, even when asked, and we allow them lots of time to make that final decision.

"We don't send them home telling them to forget. They can't forget and they need to do their grief work. We don't abandon them following the placement of the child. We stay with them as long as they want us — often attending their graduations, weddings, and the christenings of their additional children.

"But after a year or two, or three, she is able to move on to the degree that perhaps a picture and a letter from the adoptive parents on the child's birthdays and at Christmas will be enough. She tends to move aside because she wants her child to be parented by the adoptive parents. She doesn't want to interfere. We don't tell our clients this, but they sense it. They are, after all, concerned for the well-being of their children.

"The adoptive parents have the same sense. They are told so often by well-meaning friends and relatives that open adoption is risky and wrong, that if the birthparent sees the child, or even pictures of the child, she is going to want him back.

"But they soon find that the warnings aren't true. In fact, the exact opposite occurs. The more post-placement information the birthparent has and the more often she (he) has it, the less that parent thinks about challenging the relinquishment. The decision for adoption and the choice of family is confirmed and reconfirmed and a relationship develops," Magee explained. Options has never had a birthparent challenge a relinquishment.

Magee suggests that adoptive families opposed to or uncomfortable with such a degree of openness find another program or agency. About 95 percent of Options clients were actually meeting families in 1986. Some birthmothers do not want to meet the adoptive parents. However, if the family is willing to meet with her, she is more likely to choose them. She realizes they care about her, will share information later, and will tell her/their child about her and why she chose adoption.

If she doesn't want to meet the adoptive parents, or, as happens only once or twice a year, she doesn't even want to see her child, her Options counselor talks with her about it, suggesting that she may regret her decision not to do so. The counselor then takes pictures of the child and places them in the client's folder.

If she decides weeks or months later that she wants to see the pictures, they have them for her. If at that time she wants to meet the family, the adoptive parents are usually very gracious about cooperating, according to Magee. In fact, having this meeting may become very important to her sometime in the future.

Home Studies Are Extensive

Linda Brunner, who has performed many home studies for WACAP, spoke of making several visits and spending many hours with each family. "They write autobiographies and I depend heavily on reference letters," she said. "It's important when we're dealing with the girl and with the family to be open and to let girls and families search out their feelings. I like to give would-be adoptive parents an assignment in which they think about their feelings toward birthparents."

Before the study is initiated, the family attends at least two meetings with other adoptive parents. There is also required reading. WACAP provides support groups for adoptive parents and the pre-placement process is not seen as just a "study" or "screening," but also as a time of preparation for adoption and parenting. They know that adoptive parents are vulnerable too.

Mystical Bonds of Open Adoption

"What we find," Magee mused, "is when a family is chosen and the child is placed, it *is* their child in some mysterious mystical way. Adoption is different from biological parenting, but when the child comes to them, there is a tremendous bonding. We have had adoptive parents who have been chosen two or three times, and then the birthmother decided to parent — but when the adoptive family does receive a child, there is tremendous bonding.

"In the days before first names were shared, I have seen birthparents name the child and the adoptive parents give the child the name of one of the birthparents. Birthmothers appear to know. She may look at one family and say 'This is it.' Or she may look at ten or she may look at twenty, and then say, 'This is my family.'

"That family is often very like hers. But whatever the reason, the birthparents, and frequently their entire families, recognize the adoptive parents immediately."

Helen Magee concluded, "It is only the Imperial white man who has had closed adoption. Other peoples have always had open adoption. When I get nervous about what we're doing, I go back and read about Moses. His was, after all, the first recorded open adoption.

"I believe families, especially the adoptees, can deal with open adoption, but I don't believe they can live securely with secrecy and lies and pretense. I know birthparents can't. If, as we are told, adoption is a lifelong process, we need to remember that the adopted person's life begins at conception, not on the day of placement."

Leann's Story

Leann had already broken up with her baby's father when she discovered she was pregnant. She was a senior in high school and was attending beauty school at night. Her parents had divorced when she was 12, but she, her mother, and her brother were a closely-knit family.

Leann's son was born 18 months ago. She talked about her life before and after his birth:

I didn't go to the doctor until I was five months pregnant. I wasn't with the baby's father and I didn't want to be pregnant *at all*, so I didn't let myself believe it. I did a lot of crying those first few months.

My mom and I talked a lot and decided I should abort, but it was too late. We're both real glad I didn't do that. I knew from the beginning I would rather relinquish the baby for adoption.

I had a tough time at school. Kids called me names, talked about me, said I didn't even know who the father was. They'd say, "I don't see how anybody could give a baby up after carrying it for nine months. You must not love him." I told them this took a lot more love.

Caring Counselor at Options

We called two places and decided on Options because it was so open and relaxed. At Options they cared. Joanne (counselor) came over one night and talked with us. Soon after that I started looking at synopses of families because I wanted to pick one out soon. I didn't want him to stay in a foster home and I was already seven months pregnant.

The family I chose was the one most like my own family, people who enjoy doing the same things we do. This was right before Christmas, so I asked the agency to call them on Christmas Day and tell them. I think they were excited. They wrote me a letter immediately.

Joshua was born a month later. I had planned to see him only for a few minutes after his birth - that was all. I wasn't going to meet his adoptive parents either.

I saw him as planned. Then the next day some friends came to see me and we went down to the nursery to see Joshua. He had to stay in the hospital four days after I went home because his blood sugar was low. I didn't want his adoptive parents to see him until that was fixed, but I didn't want him to be alone there. So I went in and visited him every day.

Ron, my boyfriend, and I finally decided we wanted to meet the parents so I called my counselor. We decided

Mary and Toby should call me first so they did, and we talked for at least an hour. I felt like I knew them then.

My mom hadn't wanted to meet them either, but she changed her mind, too, without knowing I had. She called Joanne about it, and Mary and Toby went to see her at work.

Joshua was released Friday and they took him to a foster home first. We were to meet Mary and Toby there. When Ron and I got there, the baby was sleeping but we picked him up and both of us held him. Then I saw a car coming and I took the baby away from Ron. I was real nervous, shaking real bad. When I saw them through the window I shook even more.

Instant Bond With Adoptive Parents

Mary and Toby came in, and there was an instant bond between us that wouldn't quit. They were wonderful. I gave the baby to the mom myself.

We talked and took pictures for 45 minutes. I love unicorns and I had mentioned that in my letter. They brought me a pewter unicorn which I cherish. I showed them the photo album my mom and I put together for them with several pages of pictures of our family. We put in a picture of me when I was pregnant and my senior class picture plus a poem my mom had written. I gave the baby a unicorn rattle.

It was a wonderful meeting. The adoptive mom and I were sitting there and we would look at each other. Her husband would know we were going to cry so he'd throw in some little joke. They are the most wonderful people in the world.

I won't see the baby but I plan to see his parents. He's 18 months old now, and I have a lot of pictures of him, but I think that's all I can handle now. There are still a lot of things I want to talk about with Mary and Toby, and my grandma wants to meet them.

My mom's parents accepted all this, and we can talk about it, but not the other side of the family. With them, it's like it never happened. I've tried to talk about it but they shut me off totally. Everybody in my mom's family sees the baby pictures, reads the letters, and can share.

That first month was hard in the sense I was missing the baby. I wanted him near me, but then again, I was at ease because I got pictures and letters from Mary and Toby. Knowing that Joshua was OK, knowing what wonderful people they are meant so much. They're giving him the love he needs.

I went to an adoption support meeting one night and talked about my experience and what I went through. I let them know they aren't bad persons. A lot of people talk about how bad you are if you adopt, but there is nothing wrong with what you're doing. You're OK, I told them. I think I helped a few girls make up their minds, to know that what they were doing was not wrong.

Leann's Mother Shares Feelings

Leann's mother has been divorced for several years. She felt especially close to Leann in her decision because one of her sons is adopted. She also empathized with Leann's loss because another son died of cancer several years ago. She shared her thoughts about Leann and the adoption:

When I learned she was pregnant, initially I was angry. Why did she let this happen? I said, "I can't talk about this right now," and I went to bed. I couldn't cope with it.

The next day we started talking. Thank God the decision on abortion was not left to us. She was too far along.

We did a tremendous amount of talking about what this child would mean to us if we decided to keep him. I say "we" although throughout the whole time Leann knew it was her decision and I would stand by her. I was also very open and honest that I did not want to keep the baby. I'm a single parent and I didn't want to become the child's mother.

We spent a lot of time on the pros and cons of keeping or releasing. What goals had we set for ourselves? What would keeping the baby mean to those goals? What would that involve? Were we willing to give up those goals to keep the baby? How happy could we make that child?

We love him very much but what could we offer him in terms of true stability? We spent a great deal of time talking about that.

We decided that because of her age, because I'm a single parent, and because of the goals she has and the goals I have, a baby just didn't fit in. Keeping him would not be fair to him.

The decision was made quite early, but in fairness to Leann and the baby, we needed to talk a great deal about that decision. Decisions can be changed, but I feel strongly that if you make a decision very carefully, you can live with that decision and be comfortable with it. People ask how we can live with it. I have a stock answer: We spent a lot of time making that decision and I know we can live with it.

One of my sons is adopted, a completely closed adoption. When we were making the decision about an agency, we went first to the one where we got Stan. Then we went to Options, and we weren't ten minutes into that interview when I realized that for Leann, for me, and for the baby, I wanted open. The difference is incredible.

I have spent 17 years feeling concerned about Stan's birthparents and birthgrandparents. What must they think? They know nothing about us, about his family. They don't even know if he's alive. That must be a terrible 17 years of unknowing for them.

When Leann's baby is older, he will always know us through pictures and letters. In his biology class our son cannot answer the questions about his biological family. The baby will have some answers in that class.

The beautiful thing that came out of all our talk about the decision to adopt was that it helped Stan realize his mother didn't throw him out because she didn't love him. She anguished over it, cried over it, and she made the best decision she could for him because she wanted him to have the stability of a family. Because he saw what we were going through, he realized he was not just dumped.

My grandson's family share his life so beautifully with us and we appreciate that a great deal.

Mary and Toby's Experience

When I told Leann I was going to talk with her adoptive parents, she responded, "It sends chills up and down my spine that you're going to see them. . .I think I'm going to cry. Tell

*them I love them. They're wonderful and I couldn't have
handled this year without them."*

*Mary and Toby speak highly of Leann and her mother. Their
son is 18 months old, a lively little boy who loves to play
outside, say "No," play with his dog, and listen to stories. His
parents are in their early 30s and parenting obviously agrees
with them:*

Mary: It's been an incredible experience, something to
share with Joshua down the road.

Toby: We'd been married six years when we decided on
adoption. I had a fertility problem, and after several
surgeries, we were told the problem was not repairable. We
thought about artificial insemination, but to both of us, it
was the end result, the baby, that mattered. We felt good
about adoption from the beginning.

Mary: We called WACAP because I had heard positive
things about them. They've changed in the past couple of
years, gotten even more open than when we were there.
We talked about meeting the birthmother but it wasn't that
common then. Now it's happening a lot.

Toby: They told us four years ago when we applied that
some of the birthmothers wanted communication, and that
we might meet them. We thought it was a little scary, but
positive. About the only thing I didn't think I could handle
was the birthmother handing the baby to us. I thought that
would be so horrendously emotional I couldn't take it. But
that's exactly what happened. She handed the baby to
Mary. But when it happened, it was all right.

Mary: Leanne chose us right before Christmas, so she
told her counselor she wanted us to be told on Christmas
Day. This was her gift to us. The call came just before we
went over to my mother's house where we were
celebrating.

Toby: That was neat. Mom had called the night before
and said she wanted something a little different this time.
Instead of diving into the gifts immediately, she asked that
each person say something about past Christmases and
what the day meant to us. Mary was first, and she began
talking about Christmases in the past. She had barely
started when she burst out, *"This* is the best Christmas

yet" — and started to cry. We won't ever forget that
Christmas.

Mary: Joshua was born a month later. They called the
next day and said she "had delivered a baby boy to us."
Then we didn't have much contact for five days because he
was born with low blood sugar and he had to stay in the
hospital. Leann didn't want us to see him with tubes
attached — she wanted him to be perfect for us. But since
we weren't there, she went over and fed Joshua and bathed
him each day.

Toby: Leann had said she didn't want to meet us, but
Thursday night the counselor called and said Leann
changed her mind. We called her that night and talked for
a long time. That's how we got acquainted.

"You Have A New Son To Meet"

Mary: Joanne called the next morning to tell us Leann's
mother wanted to meet us too. We were eager to pick up
Joshua, but we went over to her work and talked with her.
That was a great experience too.

She was so supportive of Leann and of us. She wanted
to share some of her feelings, and she needed to see who
would have their baby. Her parting statement was, "Well,
I've talked long enough. You have a new son to meet."

Toby: Then we went over to the foster home. He had
been there only 30 minutes. Leann was there with her
boyfriend. He wasn't the baby's father, but he was a
wonderful support for her. In fact, they got married last
month.

We walked in and started to introduce ourselves to the
man standing there. But Mary saw Leann and the baby,
and we said to heck with the introductions. We never did
learn that man's name.

Mary: Leann put Joshua in my arms and my mind went
out the window at that moment. I couldn't even speak, I
was so overwhelmed with the excitement, that totally new
feeling of being a mother.

Toby: We stayed at least an hour, talking with Leann
and her boyfriend. We learned a lot more about Leann's
family and she had beautiful gifts for us. Two were from
her grandmother. She sent $25 to open a savings account

for Joshua. She had done this for all of her grandchildren, and even though her first greatgrandchild was leaving the family, she wanted to include him.

Mary: She also sent a lovely stitchery wall hanging for him. It said, "So tiny, so small, so loved by all," and had a blank place for his name. She sent the thread along so we could do it properly. We hung it in his room where we see it every day.

Leann also gave us a photo album with five pages of pictures of her and her family. She asked us to fill it up. When Joshua is 18, she hopes he comes back and meets with her and she can see the album then. She added that if he doesn't want to meet with her, she'll try her best to understand.

We took so many pictures that first year - it was ridiculous. I took them to a place that makes two copies, and we sent Leann most of them. She probably gets four or five for each one we send our families.

Toby: It's sad the number of people who don't have contact with the birthmother. We feel bad for them because they were deprived of something important. We have so much to tell Joshua. Even though his family gave him up, they loved him dearly. If we hadn't known Leann, how would we have answered when he asked us why she released him?

Leann's mother sent us pictures of Leann when she was one and when she was two. It's incredible how much he looks like her.

Mary: Communication has been nice, for the letters are affirming to us, too. We can write that Joshua is well taken care of and happy. Leann writes about how glad she is that Joshua is with us. Her mother says it's obvious to all the people who love Joshua that he's where God wanted him to be.

3

Closed Adoption — A Late Arrival

When open adoption is mentioned, most people ask "What's that?" In our culture today, traditional agency adoption of infants in non-related families is still likely to be closed. In most agencies, the birthparents and the adoptive parents will not have any face-to-face contact nor will they exchange each other's names and addresses. Open adoption — in which birthparents choose the adoptive parents and may have ongoing contact with them after the baby is placed — may seem weird and risky.

But *closed* adoption is a relatively new development in the United States, and has seldom even appeared elsewhere in the world. Yet, this form of adoption, this "standard practice" seems normal to many people in our culture. It's difficult to realize how recently adoption became hidden in secrecy.

Open Adoption In Early History

Adoption existed in early times. Moses is a classic example. He was sent down the river by his mother who had a specific adoptive parent in mind. She knew the king's daughter bathed in that river, and she figured Moses would have a better life if he were part of the king's family. Her plan worked. She and Moses' adoptive mother may not have sat down and had a long discussion about the openness they wanted in this adoption. His birthmother, however, made sure she maintained contact with Moses. None of this "I'll release him for adoption and forget he ever happened" business for her.

In ancient times in Greece and Rome, adoption could provide male heirs for families to whom no sons had been born. Adoption at that time was not done primarily for the benefit of the child.

Since U.S. law is based on British Common Law, no specific provision for adoption was made in our legal system before the mid 1800s. In England, adoption was not accepted because of the extreme importance placed on bloodlines.

Early in the history of the United States, children became apprentices in other families in order to learn a trade. Close relationships probably developed between these families and their apprentices similar to those within adoptive families.

During the 19th century, many children were orphaned and received institutional care. "Orphan trains" were organized to solve the problem of dealing with some of these homeless children. Hundreds of orphans from eastern states were placed on trains and sent to the middle west to be adopted by families wanting/needing children.

One account suggests the term "put up for adoption" came from this practice. When the train arrived in a town, the children would stand on a raised platform while people from the surrounding area looked them over and decided which ones they wanted. These children were "put up" for adoption.

Adoption Legislation in the United States

Legalities were not important for orphan train adoptees. But at about that same time, a few states began passing laws dealing with adoption. In 1850, Alabama law specified the right of a child to inherit from his adoptive parents. The next year Massachusetts passed an adoption statute which focused on the interests of the child. This was the beginning of the idea that adoption should enable a homeless child to be placed in a home where she would have all the rights, privileges, and responsibilities held by the parents' biological children, according to Hal Aigner, author of *Adoption in America: Coming of Age* (1986: Paradigm Press).

By 1929, every state provided for adoption within their legal system.

These early laws did not specify secrecy as part of the adoption process. Early in the 20th century, however, social workers were becoming professionalized. In the process, they were taking more and more responsibility for child placement. Since it was assumed that most children available for placement were illegitimate, and since illegitimacy at that time was considered a terrible sin, they felt it best not to share that information with adoptive parents.

At that time, also, the belief was that social traits were inherited. The son of a drunkard was likely to become a drunkard whether or not he lived with his biological father. The daughter of an unmarried mother would surely go down that same terrible path herself. Poverty was considered a genetic trait by some people.

With these beliefs, how could social workers share such information with adoptive parents? Who would adopt, in fact, if they knew the "truth"? Secrecy in adoption became more and more acceptable.

Sealed Records Become Law

The country's first sealed record laws were passed in Minnesota in 1917, only 70 years ago. For 20 years after that, few states followed Minnesota's lead. Then, in 1938, the Child Welfare League of America, which represents the mutual interests of placement agencies and other children's services, endorsed secrecy in adoption. By the late 1940s, secrecy laws had been passed throughout most of the country.

These laws were meant to protect adoptees, adoptive parents, and birthparents.

First the birthparents. The assumption was that if a young woman sinned — and she must have sinned if she had a child when she wasn't married — she wouldn't want anyone to know about it. If she relinquished her child for adoption, she was likely to have spent her pregnancy living in a maternity home for unwed mothers. In most of these homes a generation ago, visitors were discouraged, and the residents usually lived under assumed names.

When her baby was born, she was not to see it. One birthmother remembers walking to the nursery window and being noticed by a nurse. The nurse immediately pulled the curtains down so the young mother couldn't see her baby. After all, at this point she was supposed to forget about the baby and go back to her former life. Her friends were told she spent those months visiting Aunt Hannah back in Kansas.

If having a child outside of marriage was so terrible, and if it was assumed that most adopted children had unmarried birthmothers, the child needed to be protected from such information. At least, that was some of the thinking leading to the secrecy-in-adoption laws.

Advice books published in the '40s and '50s for adoptive parents actually recommended learning as little as possible about the "sordid" facts of the child's past, according to Aigner. If they didn't know about it, they wouldn't have to share it with their child.

Perhaps the most important reason for the enactment of secrecy-in-adoption laws was for the protection of adoptive parents. If the birthparent was such a bad person, it would follow that she was not to be trusted. If she learned of her child's whereabouts, she might snatch him away. Apparently adoptive parents, who were trying so hard to believe they were the "real" parents, couldn't believe they were. If they had really thought they were their child's parents, why would the birthparent be a threat?

Fear was a big factor in sealing the records. If this was done to protect the parties within the adoption triangle from each other, there had to be something to protect them against. Adoptive parents have generally been the most protective of sealed records. If those birthparents of whom they are afraid are such bad people, what does that do to the adoptee's self esteem?

In *Do I Have a Daddy? A Story About a Single-Parent Child* (1982: Morning Glory Press), a young single mother advised, "Don't tell your child his dad's a louse because that makes him half a louse." In the same vein, if the adoptive parents imply each of their child's birthparents is a louse, that makes the child a full louse...

Open adoption continued to flourish throughout the early part of this sealed record period. During the '30s and '40s, families would invite a single pregnant woman to live with them throughout her pregnancy. If all went as planned, the family would adopt the baby. The birthmother might stay in contact through the years.

The overabundance of babies in the '50s increased the power of the adoptive parents. There were more babies than there were families to adopt those babies. Secrecy appealed to adoptive parents who assumed birthparents were a low grade of people, so adoption records became ever more tightly sealed.

"I Was Sent Away"

The effect on birthmothers of all this secrecy was often devastating. Delia, a sensitive, attractive, bright suburban mother of two teenagers, was 16 and a sophomore in high school when she became pregnant in 1963. She and Joe were deeply in love and, in fact, were married ten months after their baby was born. But Delia's parents reacted harshly to the pregnancy. Delia still finds it painful to remember those months:

> During spring vacation I was sent to live with relatives in St. Louis. It was a horrible mistake. Joe and I had been going together for three years, but that made no difference. I was pregnant and I wasn't married.

My St. Louis cousin and I didn't get along at all. Luckily I found a couple who needed a babysitter, so I moved to their home. They took me to my doctor's appointments at the county hospital.

We called an adoption agency. A woman came over once and had me sign some papers. I didn't see her again until the day after my baby was born.

I knew nothing about childbirth. I had no idea the waterbag would break or what to do with contractions coming every three minutes for eight hours. Finally I asked the nurse, "When?" She replied harshly, "You've only just begun." The aloneness of that childbirth I'll never forget.

They gave me a spinal, and I watched the baby being born. When I asked to see her, they said, "Why the hell would you care?"

I was put in a room with mothers who were keeping their babies. When the women from the adoption agency came in, they asked if I knew what the baby was. When I said no, they told me I had a girl and that she was healthy. They told me to sign the papers, and they sent me home.

A year later I sent the agency a letter to give to our daughter, but it was never acknowledged. We didn't do anything else until a year ago. I was ready to scream — I just couldn't handle it. I finally got in touch with the agency and they told me a little about the family and that she was fine. They told me not to search any longer. When they close those papers, they really close them. They said there was no way they could give us a picture or anything.

I want to see her. Is she married? What does she look like? Does she think I didn't love her?

Sometimes I feel like I'm the third party looking in at my life. I can't afford really to think about it. I can't let it ruin my life.

Search Movement Affects Adoption

Innumerable other birthmothers have endured the kind of insensitivity and cruelty experienced by Delia. In fact, just a few years after Delia's heartbreaking experience, the search movement became strong enough to be noticed. Birthmothers (and birthfathers) were becoming more open about exploring their feelings of being pushed into releasing their babies for adoption. They cared for those children, and they felt a strong need to find them. They wanted to share their reasons for going along with the adoption plan.

Adoptees became incensed about the lack of control they had over their own records. Adult adoptees, they felt, were considered children in the eyes of the law. They were not allowed to know the identity of their biological parents.

Through the search movement, more people became aware of the pain felt by all parties in the adoption triangle. For most, the pain was intensified by the fact that they were denied access to information about their own lives, their children's lives, and their birthparents' lives.

The search movement helped to make society, at least part of society, understand the problems inherent in the closed adoption system. Some agencies and independent adoption services are trying, through the practice of open adoption, to make the system work better for everyone involved.

Positive Effects of Reunion

Marjorie was born about the same time as Delia's daughter. She was adopted by a minister and his wife. They didn't hide the fact she was adopted, but they had no information at all about Marjorie's birthparents.

Marjorie loved her adoptive parents, but over the years she developed a deep bitterness, almost hate, for her birthmother. Finally she talked with a social worker because she realized her pent-up rage threatened to destroy her marriage. "Some days I want to spit on her (birthmother's) face," she said vehemently. She had always thought her mother had thrown her away and didn't want her, even though her adoptive parents had been open and positive about her adoption.

The social worker listened, then shared some letters birthmothers had written to their children. After reading them, Marjorie said in surprise, "You mean she might really care for me?" The social worker suggested that Marjorie's mother might have been forced to give her up. Then the social worker shared her own experiences as a birthmother, and talked about her own love for her birthchild. She told Marjorie how much she hopes to be reunited with him.

At the end of their discussion, the social worker gave Marjorie the name of a person who helps people search for their birthchildren or birthparents. "I told Marjorie the odds were that her mother has thought about her all these years. But I also warned her to be prepared for the possibility that her birthmother might not want contact at this time," she said.

The social worker continued the story: "It took her two weeks to find her birthmother. She called her and asked, 'Was your maiden name Lorbeter?' 'Yes.' 'Did you have a child on July 15, 1963?' The woman froze for an instant, then said she did.

"Her birthmother was absolutely thrilled. She had prayed about her daughter all these years, wondered and worried about her. She had since married and had two children who don't know about Marjorie. Marjorie told her that she didn't want to disrupt her family life. But her birthmother assured Marjorie that she would tell them, and that she wants Marjorie to meet her brother and sister.

"Marjorie went from being extremely bitter to having this inner peace. And the birthmother has expressed the same kind of feeling of peace, of an important issue being settled at last," the social worker concluded.

Elaine and John Choose Secrecy

The other side of all this past secrecy is illustrated in the story of a young woman and her mother. Sara was adopted independently by Elaine and John, but they were and still are determined to keep the whole process as secretive as possible.

Elaine, a worried-looking white-haired woman, still panics, 18 years later, at the thought of her daughter's birthmother turning up:

John and I were in our late 20s when we were married. We wanted several children, but I miscarried my first three pregnancies. Finally I carried our baby seven months, and our little girl was born. She weighed only four pounds, and she died the next day. Of course we were heartbroken.

By this time, I was 36 and John was 40. We knew we probably couldn't get a child from an adoption agency because we were so old. We did call an agency here in town, but when I told her our ages, she said we should consider adopting an older child.

We wanted a baby badly, so we began the application process. The caseworker visited us here at home and asked us more questions than I dreamed possible. We were still hurting from Janie's death, and she kept asking questions about her and about my other pregnancies. The visit was very draining, and we felt defeated when she left.

We heard from the agency about six months later. She wanted to know if we wanted to keep our application current. We said yes, but I told her we were still hoping for a baby. Her sigh at our impossible request came through loud and clear.

A few months later a neighbor said she knew someone whose doctor had a patient who wanted to give up her baby. Were we interested? We thought about the risks, but decided we'd gamble. Maybe if we kept everything very secretive, it would be all right.

We talked to the doctor and called our attorney. The baby was due in two months. We already had a room ready for a baby and enough clothes to last the first year — my friends had given me a shower before Janie was born.

We waited and waited. Sara was finally born two weeks late, the longest two weeks in our lives. But she was a fine healthy baby, and we were thrilled. We brought her home from the hospital when she was five days old. Of course we never met her mother and I don't think her mother ever saw her.

Those first six months were awful. We knew every time the doorbell rang, it would be Sara's mother demanding her back. And there were times when we wondered...she had colic the first three months, and she cried for at least two hours every night. We were beside ourselves, wondering how to help her and, at the same time, dreading that visit.

But she didn't come after Sara, and six months later the adoption was finalized. We took a deep breath of relief.

Then our next door neighbor came over for coffee. She related the story of her cousin who had lost an adopted child almost a year after placement because the birthmother demanded him back. We started worrying again.

Sara graduated from high school last spring. She's had some problems, but she's working now. I still have this feeling at the pit of my stomach that her birthmother might turn up — or that Sara might search for her. But I think she has about decided not to search. We have an adopted friend who found her birthmother, and they didn't much like each other. I think Sara is fearful of what she might find if she finally met her birthmother.

And I'm still afraid of that woman.

Sara's Feelings About Adoption

Sara's version of the above story is a little different from her mother's.

My folks told me I was adopted when I was little, but they made a big deal of how this was just between them and me. I wasn't to talk about it to anyone else. They told me I was chosen, but when I got older, I realized adoption doesn't work that way. My birthmother didn't want me, and Dad and Mom wanted a baby. I'm what they got, and sometimes I think they wish they'd had a different choice.

I remember my cousin Shannon visited for a few days when I was 12 and she was 13. She knew I was adopted, of course, and she thought it was pretty neat. She told me it must be nice to know you aren't an accident. She was born several years after her parent's "first" family, and I guess she got tired of being told she was an afterthought.

We were talking about it while we were outside playing. After Shannon went back home, a little girl in our neighborhood came to our door and asked my mother if it was true that I was adopted. Mom seemed flustered and didn't answer her directly.

Later I heard her talking with Shannon's mother on the phone. She asked what Shannon had said to the neighbor kids. Then I heard her tell my aunt about the little girl asking about my adoption. I didn't understand why it was such a big deal.

Whenever my mom sees an article about an adoptee finding his birthmother, she shows it to me — if the article says the reunion wasn't a good one. I have never talked to her about wanting to find my birthmother. I know it would upset her, and I don't care that much. But I've always wondered why she gave me up. I suppose she didn't want me.

Another Birthmother's Story

For both Sara and her mother, the missing birthmother is a shadowy figure who must be up to no good. Unless they find her, they will never know.

It's possible, however, that Sara's mother feels much like Bridgit, a birthmother who wants very much to meet with her son. Bridgit felt she had no choice but adoption when her son was born in 1962. She was an honor student when she became pregnant. She dropped out of school without anyone realizing her reason.

When she tried to go back to school the next fall, the principal asked why she had missed those months of classes. She told him, and he responded in horror, "Don't you know you can never come back to school? You'd contaminate the other girls!" Bridgit's story is true, and may be quite similar to Sara's birthmother's life:

I was an honor student and a good girl. I only had sex with this guy three times, and he wanted to marry me. How could this have happened? It was such an unreal situation — I tried to deny it. I had decided I didn't want to get married, so I didn't tell him I was pregnant. I wanted this child to have a better opportunity than we could give him.

I finally told my mother at six months. She said, "Well, we'll work it out together." She assumed we would keep the baby. I went along with her for awhile, but my thoughts kept nagging me. My brothers all had IQs over 140, but they weren't doing anything with their lives, and somehow I knew they were on a downward spiral. Love alone wasn't enough. I wanted my child to have a better chance.

At about eight months, I told my aunt. She knew we were absolutely destitute so she took me to an adoption agency. I tried to consider adoption because I respected my aunt, but this caseworker turned me off completely. She was awful. She implied this baby was a commodity — "You have already sinned, and your punishment is you do not get to raise this child. You have no rights, no needs to be considered."

I asked if I could have any information about the family. She said they would tell me how long the adoptive couple had been married, how many kids they had, and their religion. Nothing else.

I asked, "Do they like music? Do they have a sense of humor?" She told me I had no choices. In 1962 the law of supply and demand was reversed to what it is today — there were not enough adoptive families for the available babies. I think the agency thought they were doing me a favor by being willing to take this baby off my hands.

But I couldn't do that. That was defeating the purpose for which I was placing my child. I was placing him out of love, not punishment, and I had to know more about his parents.

My son was born a month premature. He weighed five pounds so he stayed in the hospital two weeks. I kept him at home for two weeks after that.

Bridgit Decides On Adoption

I'd hold him and talk to him those two weeks. I told him over and over why I had to let somebody else raise him, someone who could give him a better chance at doing something with his life, someone who could provide the education I knew I couldn't afford.

I had to know where he would be. I spent my last $20 to take him to a studio to get a picture of him which I have saved all these years.

My aunt told me the minister at her son's church in Nashville wanted to adopt a baby. I figured I'd at least know where he was, and I knew I had no other choice that would be good for him. So on my seventeenth birthday my aunt agreed to drive me to Nashville where I placed my son. I met with them first, and then we took the baby to their house. They said his name would be Kenny. I kissed him, then put him in her arms in their living room and said, "Go to your new mom."

Kenny's adoptive parents agreed that I could have information about him, that they would write me a letter once in a while. But I didn't hear and I didn't hear, so I hitchhiked back to Tennessee and they took me out to dinner and told me he had blue eyes and liked his bath. They also told me not to come back any more.

Adoptive Parents Refuse Contact

Occasionally through the years until he was 14 I sent Kenny birthday cards in a second envelope addressed to his adoptive parents. They could keep it and give it to him later if they wished. On his first birthday I had a bakery cake made with roses on it, and I still have those roses, frozen. I have lived all over the United States and Europe, but I still have those roses.

Finally, when he was 14, I called them. His father got on the phone and really chewed me out. He said he hoped I'd have the decency not to contact them again.

When I graduated from Harvard I sent an announcement with a two-line note because I thought they would want to know.

Then I started working for an adoption agency and I thought Kenny's parents would be pleased. I had my director write a letter. He explained that I was a professional social worker now and that both my elderly mother and I would like to contact Kenny. Because I cared, I was going through a third party.

It was a very warm letter, but we got an extremely cold note back. They said the "boy" had had a lot of problems and it would not be in his best interest to meet me for a long time. Almost as an afterthought, they assured me that my son's problems were not related to the adoption. I appreciated that comment.

I wanted to call Kenny on his 21st birthday, but decided that was a very special day and I didn't want to risk jeopardizing his happiness.

Then last fall when Kenny turned 23, a friend who is an adoptive father called and said, "Kenny, this is Tom and you don't know me, but my wife and I are friends of a very special lady who is your birthmother. Although she knows where you are and would appreciate contact with you, she doesn't wish to intrude in any way in your life if you're not ready. She has asked me to be the mediator."

At first Kenny was a little distant, perhaps shocked, as if someone else were in the room. Then it sounded like that person had walked out, and he said he'd like me to write him.

I spent the whole weekend writing this four-page letter trying to explain as much as I could. Two friends read it and they said it was probably too much for a 23-year-old man to handle initially.

So I put the letter aside and said, "Dear Kenneth, I spent the entire weekend writing a four-page letter but decided I should wait until I know what questions you would like to ask. Please let me know if you desire further contact. I'm open to writing, phone calls, or meeting. I don't wish to intrude in your life, but I want to welcome you into mine on your terms now or at a later date. Enclosed are two of your baby pictures." I signed it, "Sincerely with love, your birthmother." Then I saved the other letter in case he wants to read it.

I don't know whether Kenny got the letter. I sent it registered mail with a return receipt requested, but I have no idea whether he signed it himself. I'm disappointed that he hasn't replied, but the phone call was wonderful. That's the important thing, that I know he's all right and he knows I care.

I still don't regret the adoption. Otherwise I couldn't be an adoption social worker now.

Once I made the approach and gave Kenny the opportunity to call me, I had this tremendous sense of inner peace. I had finally completed my obligation to him. Now he has the choice of contacting me. It's like I can finally close the door and have this inner peace. I can go on with my own life now.

Delia, Elaine, Sara, Bridgit — four women wanting something they don't have. Delia feels it's not the right time to search for the daughter she longs to see.

Elaine would give the world to have the peace of mind of knowing that Sara is truly "hers" without being haunted by her fear of Sara's birthmother.

Sara loves her mother very much, but is feeling disconnected and rootless for reasons she can't understand. She wonders if meeting her birthmother might help resolve those feelings.

Bridgit may be the lucky one in this group. She has suceeded in locating her son and, much as she would like to meet him, has decided to wait a little longer before making another effort at a reunion. But she knows it will happen when he's ready. Bridgit's fears have subsided because she knows where her son is, and she knows he's all right.

Elaine's fears may never go away. The ghost of Sara's birthmother may always haunt her unless...is it possible that if Sara found her birthmother, the reality might be the best antidote for Elaine's fears?

If Sara's birthmother could have met Elaine and John when she delivered Sara, if she could have satisfied herself that she wanted her child reared in their home, a great deal of pain might have been prevented for each person in this adoption triangle. We'll never know.

We do know the history of adoption is still being written. It appears that over time, secrecy may be written out of the adoption script. The Delias, the Elaines and Johns, the Saras and the Bridgits of the future may be dealing with far fewer ghosts. Dealing with people is generally pleasanter than battling ghosts.

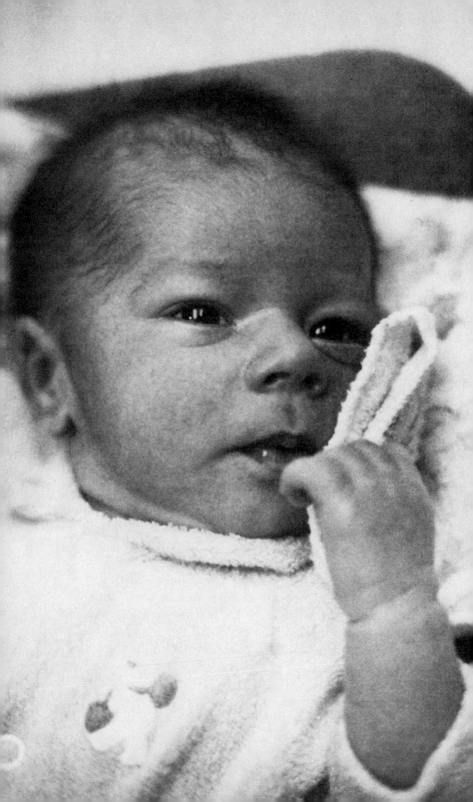

4

Calvary Chapel — Church-Connected Adoption

"We don't place babies. Birthparents place babies," firmly declared Claire Priester, a small quiet woman who exudes trust. She is the counselor for the adoption service offered by House of Ruth, Calvary Chapel, Downey, California. Openness has always been an integral part of their service.

The church's adoption ministry was started in 1979 by Karyn Johnson, wife of the minister at Calvary Chapel. One day Janice Blume, the school principal, came to her to discuss how best to help a student who was pregnant. The question brought back vivid memories for Johnson.

She, too, had been pregnant at 16. She had been convinced adoption was her only "solution," so she contacted an agency. After her child was born, she signed the relinquishment papers, and was told filing generally took about a month. During that time she understood she could change her mind and stop the adoption.

After days of agonizing indecision, she decided she could not give up her baby. She went back to the agency 24 days after signing, assuming she could have her child. She learned to her horror that her baby had already been placed with a family. There was no way the adoption could be stopped.

"I always tried to find my daughter," she related. "I begged the agency over and over to give me information, but they would not. Finally I paid a search consultant $250 and he found her. I didn't contact her until she was 18, and now we have a very good relationship. I'm her birthmother and they're her parents, and it has worked out well."

She hadn't yet searched for her daughter in 1979, but Johnson knew she wanted to help that young pregnant woman avoid the kind of hurt she was still experiencing. She and Blume talked for hours. They decided they wanted to offer some positive options to this teenager.

They knew that at that time nearly all agency adoptions in California were closed — the birthparent could not meet or even know very much about her child's adoptive parents. They knew about independent adoption, but they were uncomfortable about the risks of simply calling a lawyer and saying, "Look, our friend is about to have a baby. Can you place it with a suitable family?"

They knew the law in California specified that independent adoption referred to the baby being placed by the birthparents with the adoptive parents. But they also knew that in reality, birth and adoptive parents going through independent adoption generally did not communicate with each other any more than they might in agency adoption.

Open Adoption Plan Is Developed

The young woman was interested in adoption, but she didn't like the stories she was hearing about placing her child and never seeing him again. The two women decided to help her work out something not quite so hurtful.

They found several couples interested in adopting a child. They explained the situation to them and they agreed to let the young birthmother meet them. She chose one of the couples, and after delivery, placed her child with them. They agreed to exchange letters and pictures with her, and have continued to do so, although infrequently after the first year.

Because this was such a positive thing, Johnson and Blume felt a sense of guidance, of starting a ministry in this area. They felt that a lot of the doubt and guilt and trauma associated with giving a child up for adoption was a result of the closed system generally followed in both agency and independent adoption.

They decided they wanted to provide something that could be helpful to all parties. The open adoption was to make the whole process as positive as possible for the birthmother. It would also help adoptive parents be better parents because they would be able to answer more of their child's questions. This in turn would help the child accept her adopted status.

In 1979 this was not popular. When the ministry began, they were afraid of the long-term implications of certain expressions of openness, according to Johnson. They walked softly and cautiously and tried new things along the way. "Birth and adoptive parents understanding one another is the key," she pointed out. "Birthparents need to understand the needs of adoptive parents and adoptive parents must empathize with the pain that birthparents feel.

"Of course open independent adoptions had been happening for years in California, but this was not really popular because we had been socialized to protect the adoptive parents from those awful birthparents who would come and prey on them if they knew them. But we have found we can help them develop a relationship where all parties respect one another."

Service Grows Rapidly

In 1985 the adoption service, designed specifically for birthparents who prefer a born-again Christian couple to parent their child, assisted in the placement of 42 babies, half again as many as in the preceding year. During the first couple of years they helped place six or seven. Then, as their policies became known, more and more women came to them for pregnancy counseling.

Priester, who became the counselor for the adoption service two years ago, basically is against closed adoption. However, if someone comes in and says she doesn't want to meet the family, she doesn't have to do so. But since it is not legal for an adoption service (as distinguished from a licensed agency) to choose the family, they take the pictures off the descriptive files of adoptive parents. Then the birthparent is asked to read the files and choose a family. They also pursue it as a counseling issue. Why does she not want to meet the adoptive parents? What is she hiding? What does she fear?

"We see a lot of people who want to adopt a baby but who don't like the idea of open adoption. They want to work with us because we know girls who have babies, but they are threatened by the whole idea of openness," Priester explained.

"I think this has several reasons — one is a real selfishness, a lack of sensitivity to the needs of others. The other is non-acceptance of their own infertility. You don't feel good about not having your own children, so you want to pretend this adopted child is your own. I can understand this, but when I hear a couple who are in that position, I tell them I don't think they're ready yet for a child."

Information Provided in Seminar

Adoptive parent applicants pay a $75 fee to attend an all-day seminar. They meet in the sanctuary of Calvary Chapel. Typically, speakers include staff members, a lawyer, birthmothers, adoptive parents, and generally a couple who went through the infertility testing and decided against adoption.

The seminar is designed to remove some of the fears participants may have about open adoption. This may be the first time they have actually met birthparents, young people who are not terrible persons after all, young people who want a good life for their babies.

If the couple is still interested in adoption after the seminar, they pay a $300 "start file" fee. In addition, they pay any pregnancy-related expenses to the birthmother which may include medical bills (if she has no or only partial insurance).

They prepare their resume complete with pictures, hobbies, reasons they want a child, etc. Each birthparent may look through as many of these files as she wishes, and may interview one or more couples. After she makes her decision, she may see the couple occasionally until the baby is born. Degree of contact after delivery varies with the people involved, but the key, according to Priester, is trust in each other. It seems to work.

Services are tailored to the needs of each birthparent. "We look at her support system — how wise and capable are those who are close to her? Then we try to supply through counseling what she lacks in that support system.

"We are a temporary part of her life. In fact, if she is a very young girl, I may work more with her mom because she will still be there when I'm gone," Priester added.

Birthfather's Role

The birthfather's involvement is always welcomed. When the birthmother first calls, she is asked, "Where is the birthfather in this? Does he know you are pregnant? Is he interested in adoption? Would you like to bring him in?"

If she says "No," Priester explains the legal problems involved. His signature is needed as well as hers in order to place the child with another family. "In a few cases girls have been able to get away with not naming the father. We obviously cannot force her to declare him, but we talk about the legal risks and how it may be more difficult to find adoptive parents interested in taking this risk.

"Normally it is comforting to know that nothing really demanding is required of him. Sometimes mailing a letter

with a waiver of notice which must be notarized is
enough. This letter explains his rights and the meaning of
the waiver of notice. It gives the birthfather an
opportunity to say he wants nothing more to do with the
situation.

"In all cases, after the baby is born and is in the home
of the adoptive couple, the social worker sends a letter to
him saying, 'The baby has been born and you are the
declared father. Here are your options.' If he does nothing,
doesn't even respond to the certified letter," Priester
explained, "abandonment proceedings are initiated and his
rights are terminated. If he wishes to prevent the
adoption, he must take legal action unless the birthmother
or adoptive parents decide to pull out."

Most birthfathers wind up being cooperative, however,
according to Priester. "If we give him a chance to work
through his feelings, to get angry, to say, 'No way are you
taking my baby,' he lets us explain how adoption can be.
Usually he has this totally out of control picture of
adoption, that he has no power, and he is reacting to that.
He needs to have a chance to talk about it and to take a
look at their life situation. He's likely to see that he is not
ready to parent.

"Most guys are reasonable and they usually come to the
same conclusion the birthmother did if they are treated
like human beings. Ignoring them, however, can cause
problems," Priester concluded.

Lawyers Carefully Selected

Many professionals in the adoption field believe the
birthparent and the adoptive parents need separate
lawyers. If only one is used, that lawyer may be partial to
the rights of the adoptive parents because they are paying
the bill. Priester does not believe this is necessary.

"We find lawyers who are also strongly for the rights of
the birthmother and compassionate about her needs," she
explained. "If in his eyes this is just a baby, it will not

work. This is a very vulnerable issue, and each person, and especially the birthparents, must be treated with tender loving care."

Obviously the lawyer must also be someone who is impeccably honest. Having only one lawyer is legal in California because there is no conflict of interest, according to Priester. Although the bill is paid by the adoptive parents, they are working together for the welfare of the child.

Priester also discussed the thorny problem of the adoptive parents paying expenses, and then the birthmother deciding to keep her child to parent herself. Must she pay that expense money back?

"If this happens, the money is a donation," Priester explained. "Legally, any money given to the birthparents must be considered a gift of charity. You don't ask for it back just as you can't ask for a refund from the church or United Way. Otherwise you would be paying for the baby and that is baby-buying. That's illegal.

"Sometimes she says to me, 'What if I accept this money for my expenses, and then I change my mind?' I reply, 'Well, that's one of the reasons we want you to examine this issue as completely as you can so you won't be the bad guy. But sometimes you do have to change your mind, and if that's the case, you aren't required to pay them back.' Usually she says, 'Oh my gosh, I'd feel terrible about that.' But we make sure the adoptive parents know that's the risk they take.

"These birthmothers — it's not just the hurt of losing their babies, but they don't want to hurt the adoptive parents. If a pregnant woman comes in who sounds a bit calloused about the needs of the adoptive parents, sometimes I say, 'You know, maybe you would like to work with a lawyer.' I have turned down two girls in the two years I have worked here."

Stephanie's Story

Stephanie released her baby for adoption ten months ago with help from Claire Priester at Calvary Chapel. She still has days when she grieves over the baby she placed with Carole and Brian. But she is enthusiastic about open adoption, and finds that writing letters to the baby helps her cope with her sadness.

I was barely 17 when I got pregnant and I was devastated. I just didn't think it would happen to me, and I took it hard. My mother handled it remarkably well. She mentioned adoption but she said she would help if I decided to keep it.

First we contacted an agency, then a lawyer, but I didn't like either one. A friend recommended Calvary Chapel so I called. Claire came over immediately. She was concerned for me, and helped me make my decision.

I decided open adoption was the best thing for me, so my sister and I went over there to look at their files. Claire said I could see as many as I wanted. We read them all and picked out three of them that I liked.

Not long afterward, when I was about five months pregnant, I interviewed them all, about an hour per couple. Claire was there with me. At first I didn't know what to ask and she helped me. One question she asked them was, "Describe your husband" — and he was sitting right there. When Carole heard that one, she started crying and said, "Well, he's my Prince Charming," and I thought, "These are the people."

Claire and I went out to lunch with Carole and Brian. At first it was awkward, and then we started talking about our plans for the baby. They promised to send me pictures and said I could see her occasionally. I liked them a lot.

Carole and I went shopping a few times. Once we went into a baby store to look at cribs and all the other neat things I could have. I started crying, and Carole started crying, and we got out of there.

We went out to lunch several times, Claire, Carole, and me. We went to the hospital to look at the rooms. I wanted Carole to be with me when I delivered, but I wanted my mom, too, because she was feeling left out for awhile.

They weren't with me after all because I had a C-section.

I thought about my decision all during my pregnancy, so I had a straight plan as to what I was going to do. People would ask me if I was sure. I said, "Sure, I'm not ready to be a mother, and I think my baby needs a father."

Bittersweet Hospital Experience

The hospital staff was great. They knew what I was doing and they followed my orders — which almost caused a problem. I had said I didn't want to see my baby but I changed my mind. So I held her, but I think Carole and Brian got to hold her right after she was born. Actually I think they were with her more than I was. I really didn't understand that the baby was allowed to come into my room and I could have held her and fed her. I wish now I had.

When they came in to pick up the baby that third day, that was the worst. I knew she was leaving, and I thought I would never see her again (that was my plan at the time). That was so emotional, saying goodbye to her, almost like talking to someone who was going to die.

Then I went to my room and I started crying. All those thoughts going through my mind — I want her back, I don't want this. But my mom was there and so was Claire. They helped a lot.

I stayed in the hospital that night and went home the next day. It was really tough. Because I had a C-section, I was supposed to stay two more days, but I didn't want to be there if the baby was gone. I felt fine although it was hard to walk.

Intense Grieving Period

The next few weeks were hard, a lot of crying. I called Claire a few times and she came over. I talked to another girl who had given her baby up. We cried on the phone, and she told me it was normal. You have got to have somebody tell you it's normal, that this is not going to continue all your life. You're going to get through it, and what you did was right.

These feelings were strong, but it was a short period, crying all the time, thinking my world was coming to an end. I remember crying a lot for about a month. Then I went back to work and that helped.

Having somebody to talk to helps. Writing letters to the baby helps. I wrote two or three letters telling her how I felt, and that helps because you feel like you're talking to her and explaining why you did it. That really helped me know it was the right decision.

Good Relationship With Adoptive Parents

I'm glad I know Carole and Brian. I would never change that. You have to have that security. I don't know how a person could give up her baby to just anybody. I have wondered about that. That baby is in their hands and you need to know what kind of people they are. I even thought a few times that I could never change my mind and hurt these people — but that can't be the reason you decide on adoption, of course.

I saw Carole and Brian when Meghan was two months old, and again a couple of months ago. The last time they wrote, about a month ago, they told me she was walking, getting in the toilets, splashing the water around. They sent several pictures, and she's beautiful.

They told me I could see Meghan again when she's a year old. I'd love to see her to see how she acts, to compare her with me. Of course she doesn't know who we are and that hurts. I was just a nobody. She didn't want me touching her, didn't want me feeding her, and that hurt. Carole worked so hard to make me feel comfortable.

I don't want them to feel like every six months they have to bring her over to my house. They have to live their own lives. Sometimes I think, why can't we be friends? Why can't they visit like anyone else? But it's not the same. We both have something in common, we share someone we both love very much. But I don't want to make them feel uncomfortable. If bringing the baby over or having me visit makes them uncomfortable, I don't want to do that to them.

I think I'll wait until the papers are final, and then I'll write and ask if I can see Meghan. But I feel like I'm wanting this to go on forever. I guess that's one thing to which I'll never have an answer.

Carole and Brian — Heartbreak of Infertility

When I visited Carole and Brian, Meghan, a tiny blonde 10-month-old dynamo, was happily practicing her recently acquired walking skills. For awhile she played peek-a-boo with me by "hiding" behind a little lace doiley. Then, clutching the doiley, she toddled over to her dad, stumbled, was up again instantly, then grabbed his knee. He picked her up, hugged her, then kissed her little button nose.

Carole and Brian have been married for nine years. They planned to have two children, but decided to wait a few years. Five years after their wedding they figured it was time — but nothing happened. Carole didn't get pregnant. After two years they started infertility testing. They share their story:

Brian: We thought we were being responsible those five years we weren't ready to have children. Then we decided we'd been pretty stupid practicing birth control when we didn't need to.

Carole: The whole emotional thing — you have to keep your sense of humor through all this.

Brian: The tests certainly are not glamorous. We tried the temperature route, taking it every morning. For awhile there seemed to be some possibility of getting pregnant — that if we did everything right...your sex life gets real mechanical at this point.

Since I'm the one who apparently can't have children, I forced myself to consider it (infertility) real seriously because I didn't want to find one day that I hadn't thought about it and it was a heavier thing than I had realized. Perhaps it hit me with the same intensity it would anybody, but for a very short period of time. Probably in my mind I resolved that the Lord had some purpose in it, and there was no sense crying over something He has promised is for my ultimate good. It was terribly hard for me, but I have known other people who have had a lot more trauma to deal with.

Carole: At the time it seemed like a big deal.

Brian: What made it seem like a big deal is that, although I still believe in miracles, it's pretty permanent ...if you lose your house or your car blows up or you're fired, you always know you can get another car or another house or job, but this was not going to change. It hit me that the bloodline ends here. But it didn't cripple me — the pain didn't last long. And when Meghan arrived, any misgivings I had disappeared. I figured no child born to us could be as beautiful as she is.

The Adoption Decision

When we decided we wanted to adopt, we went to the county first, and they told us it would be a six to eight year wait for a newborn Caucasian, but probably less than a year if we wanted an older child.

We had some friends who adopted a child through House of Ruth, so we called Claire and went to their seminar. They presented the perspective of the birthparents and also some parents who decided not to adopt and who had children of their own. They also explained to us what they were trying to do, that their first priority was wanting to help the birthparents. They wanted to be sensitive to our needs but we were second on the totem pole.

They also suggested other ways of adopting — foreign adoption or through attorneys. A lot of people blitzed the market, put their names on the county lists, saw attorneys, but we decided to put all our eggs in one basket — House of Ruth.

Carole: I think that seminar showed us the different emotions and personalities of birthmothers that we hadn't thought of before. You think of this nonentity, this birthmother, this non-person. Then when we started considering these options — degrees of openness — we realized, yes, she is a person, a person who may not be able to keep her child but wants her child in a home with two parents.

Importance of Counseling

Brian: After Stephanie chose us and we met her, my thought was that I was so glad that when she had her child, someone would still be there. We knew that after we adopted, we wouldn't want to find time to be a constant friend of hers, too. We were glad House of Ruth was helping her through the sorrow she would feel. Our hearts really went out to her.

Carole: Eventually we thought about the hurt for the whole family — the grandmother because this was her first grandchild, and the emotions she went through. Claire helped us realize there are people at the other end of the adoption, not just a piece of paper you sign and it's all over by the next morning.

After Stephanie chose us, she and I went shopping several times. We went to some LaMaze classes together, but Meghan ended up being a C-section baby so we couldn't help. But it was neat — I won't ever do that ·

Brian: Stephanie called us for an interview nearly three months before Meghan was born, but we didn't buy any baby furniture. We didn't want to because we knew that sometimes things fall through. We bought Meghan two outfits to take to the hospital. Then we took her with us when we went out to buy furniture.

Claire told us they had had only one or two birthmothers in the previous year who, after going through their counseling, decided not to release after the baby was born. That's why we were afraid of referrals from attorneys — those birthparents seldom had any counseling. Claire said they certainly could make no guarantee, but we thought the counseling made a big difference.

I understand that if a girl comes in who is absolutely certain she wants to place her baby, she still is expected to go through a lot of counseling. After Meghan was born, Stephanie didn't want to give her up. I think before delivery she hadn't expected it to be a problem — she didn't want kids and she didn't want to think about keeping her. But after she was born, of course she looked at Meghan and thought, "This beautiful little thing, I'd love to keep her. I don't want to give her up." But her reasons for giving her up were still there. Emotionally, it was very hard for her.

Even in the hospital we tried to keep our emotions in hand, still thinking of Meghan as Stephanie's baby. Even when we brought her home we thought, do we call

ourselves Mommy and Daddy yet? But we figured if
Stephanie had gone this far she must be committed to
giving Meghan to us.

While we were in the hospital we tried to put some sort
of wall to it so we wouldn't be too hurt. At House of Ruth
they impressed on us that we must be prepared for the
possibility that things could change. They also asked how
we would respond if the baby was born with missing
fingers or something. They asked, "Are you going to say,
'Oh, this baby is not a perfect baby, we don't want her?'"
We pretty much made up our minds that this would be
like our biological child and we would accept her
unconditionally.

Advantages of Open Adoption

Carole: One thing I appreciate about open adoption is
that if Meghan ever has any medical problems, we can go
directly to her birthmother for information, and I feel good
about that. Meeting her birthmother, knowing what type of
person she is, whether she is tall or short, her background
— I think it will be good for Meghan to know.

Brian's sister Nancy was adopted and she doesn't know
anything much about her background. She has some
health problems, and the doctors say if we knew more
about her family's health history, they might be able to
help her more.

Brian: I think open adoption is more traumatic
emotionally until the adoption is final. But then I think it's
much better because we can tell Meghan in honesty that
she was loved. I hear so many adopted people say they
must not have been loved. My parents really don't know
for my sister. They have to assume her birthparents loved
her.

But we can say to Meghan, "Your mommy loved you. We
have a picture of her holding you and we know she loves
you — in fact, so much so that the choice she made was
for you and not for her. Her desire would have been just
to keep you." I think that's a big plus and a big benefit to
Meghan.

I don't think I'll feel intimidated if Meghan wants to
know Stephanie in later years. But in my sister's situation,

my parents don't know what's out there, and they imagine first that her birthparents must not love her, but at the same time they think they might try to snatch her out of their arms. I know that wouldn't be the situation at all with Stephanie and Meghan.

I think a big part of our decision-making and being able to cope with whatever happens is that we are Christian and we know the Lord is in control. If Stephanie had changed her mind a month or so later, we could have accepted that...but not now!

Carole: A lot of it is just taking it a day at a time and seeing how things evolve. Right now we have gone a little further than we thought we would at first.

Open adoption is a new thing, and when you are dealing with options, you take it one step at a time. Just like Meghan learning to walk, we're taking open adoption one step at a time. We really don't know what we'll do in the next ten years.

Brian: I think there will be a stage, perhaps when Meghan is three or four years old, when a meeting with Stephanie might confuse her. That's when we might say, "Let's don't meet right now."

Carole: It was kind of awkward at first because I would think, I wonder what Stephanie would think about this. I don't want her to think I'm a bad parent. I wanted so much to be the kind of parent she wanted me to be. Now I learn as I go and do the best I can.

I think we're open-minded people, but Meghan is our main concern. We're learning, Stephanie is learning. We're trying to work together to keep everybody happy. I don't really have a final answer as to how things are going to be in the next few years.

Brian: When people ask if next time we'd want closed adoption or another baby from House of Ruth, I respond that closed adoption wouldn't be for us. If we didn't meet her, we would probably think of the birthmother as some kind of monster, and she would think the same about us.

With Meghan we can say, "We have met your mom, we have pictures of her." I think that will mean a lot. Now that we have survived some of the emotional trauma, I think it's been worth it to provide that for her.

5

Birthparents/Adoptive Parents — Tender Loving Care Required

Most characters in the adoption drama have had a rough time. Usually it's the birthmother alone with little or no support system who suffers the most. But nearly everyone involved in an adoption plan will, or already has faced hurt, depression, and the loss of dreams.

One of the most important keys to successful adoption is working with a third party who doesn't consider him/herself in charge. The birthparent and the adoptive family are in charge, and the counselor is simply the facilitator, the one who helps the process along.

People who feel powerless when they make a decision will always wonder if they made the right decision. The birthparent who sees no way she can rear her child herself feels absolutely powerless if her adoption plan is dictated by someone else. The adoptive parents feel powerless as they fail to conceive and endure infertility testing to no avail.

Open adoption allows all parties to be deeply involved. But power must be shared. The counselor can help each party understand the needs of the others as they work toward an agreement acceptable to all.

Birthfather's Role In Adoption

Even if the birthparents are together and decide they are not ready to be parents, making an adoption plan and carrying it through will be difficult. One or the other may not agree with the plan. Each may blame the other for making adoption seem necessary.

More often, however, the birthparents are not together. For whatever reasons, they know they will not parent this child as a team. The birthmother in this situation may feel abandoned. She may think adoption is a poor alternative, but feels she has no other choice. She needs family support and good counseling services as she works through the hardest decision she will ever make in her life.

Some fathers may skip out on the whole thing, may even refuse to acknowledge paternity. "It's not my baby," he says. Even these fathers are likely to feel grief, remorse, and/or guilt at some point. Each knows he has a child somewhere, a child he refused to accept.

Another birthfather will want to be involved with his baby and may pressure the birthmother to keep the baby. He may say, "If you don't want it, I'll take it." Yet, the birthmother knows he has no more resources for parenting the child than she does.

These fathers are likely to experience grief over the loss of the child, and perhaps guilt for not assuming this responsibility. They, too, need counseling to help them deal with their realities. In Chapter 11, a birthfather shares his guilt and his sadness over his daughter's adoption.

Whether or not the birthfather is involved in the decision-making, his signature is needed on the adoption papers. He has three choices. He may give his permission, as the birthfather, for the adoption to proceed. He may sign a statement denying he is the father of this child. Or he may sign away his rights to this child — which neither acknowledges nor denies paternity.

If he cannot be found, abandonment proceedings may be carried out. The law and the interpretation of these laws vary from state to state. In adoption proceedings, it is extremely important to obtain the father's cooperation or for the court to declare his rights waived.

Adoptive Parent Dilemma

"Traditionally, adoption agencies have tended to assume there were no real counseling issues with adoptive parents. All they needed to make them well was a baby," commented Janet Cravens-Garner, Lutheran Social Service of Texas. She pointed out that the couple first must come to terms with their impaired fertility. In addition, they must deal with several other important issues.

"Adopters must accept some cold hard facts about their lives and their relationships," Cravens-Garner said. "They will never be complete parents in the sense of having this child born to them. Their adopted child has another set of parents, a genetic heredity. The adoptive parents need to make peace with the fact that their family is different.

"The adoptive parents also must develop empathy for their child's birthparents — not just all birthparents, but the specific couple who gave birth to their child.

"In fact, there are many counseling issues with adoptive parents which are just as intimate and intense as the birthparent issues," Cravens-Garner concluded. She does not feel most people who facilitate adoptions are doing enough to help adoptive parents deal with these issues.

But by the time the adoptive parents have their child, they are positive that parenting this baby will be the most wonderful thing they have ever experienced. Their greatest dream is finally realized.

Yet they still need tender loving care and understanding at this time. Hopefully, they have already worked through the above issues, but they may experience post-partum blues in much the same way a biological mother does. They are probably very tired. Aren't all new parents?

The anxiety they feel if the adoption is not yet final is overwhelming. What if the birthparents decide to keep

him after all? See chapter 7 for a discussion of the
possibility of disrupted adoption.

One adoptive mother reported she felt as though she
was babysitting the first few weeks. "I kept thinking, is
this how Susan would do it? I wanted her to think I was a
good mother," she said.

Adoptive parents may think open adoption robs them of
any power in their adoption plan since they generally are
chosen by the birthparent. But they have the power to say,
"No, this doesn't feel right to us." It's important, as an
adoptive mother expressed it, not to feel desperate.

The counselor can help the adoptive couple understand
that in open adoption they may and should be involved in
setting up the contact agreement with the birthparents. If
they don't want much contact, they should make this
clear. Some birthparents will agree with them.

Brian and Carole, who adopted Stephanie's baby, and
who shared their story in chapter 4, felt they had choices.
Brian said:

> Once, after we gave them our application, they said there
> was a baby available, but we had to decide that day. It was
> somebody they had not worked with before delivery. We
> decided not to be involved that time.
>
> What House of Ruth did that we appreciated was the
> counseling with Stephanie. Number one, we knew she had
> not been pushed or coerced, and number two, we had
> some sensitive questions we could ask through Claire. We
> didn't want to be insensitive, but we have feelings too.

Understanding Birthmother's Grief

The person hurting the most in an adoption is the
birthmother. It is she who carried this baby for nine
months. Bonding between mother and baby starts during
pregnancy, and breaking that bond is painful.

But her hurt probably started long before the baby was
born. Several of the young women profiled in this book
spoke of breaking up with their boyfriends before they

even realized they were pregnant. The shock of finding she's pregnant, facing her family and friends, and knowing the baby's father is already out of the picture is harsh indeed. No wonder she may try to ignore for as long as possible the fact that she's pregnant.

If she considers adoption, the baby's father needs to be involved. She may feel very strongly that she never wants to see him again. Looking for him, telling him about her adoption plans, getting him to sign the papers would be extremely difficult for her.

Perhaps her counselor can do the actual contacting of the birthfather. The birthmother's help may be needed to locate him, but her feelings should be respected as much as possible in this painful situation.

Broken Dreams

Having the father gone when she discovers she's pregnant, the cold turkey approach, is hard. It may be even harder to lose the father during pregnancy. Sonia reported:

> Jim and I had dated since eighth grade, and I got pregnant at the end of tenth. We were planning to get married — the high school romance. Karen was basically planned — I wanted to get pregnant. I hadn't used birth control for a year, and we were excited. We had already planned to get married. Then, because of the pregnancy, we were going to be married sooner. He was going to move in with me at my grandma's house where I was living.
>
> But at about 4½ months, he decided the baby wasn't his. He was starting his senior year in high school, and I think the responsibility scared him. He had a good job but he didn't think he could handle having a family right away. I went back to high school after I had the baby, and our lockers were close to each other. He wouldn't look at me. A friend tried to show him a picture of the baby, and he wouldn't even glance at it.

Another young woman who said her baby was planned
was Londa:

> I really wanted to keep my baby. Before I got pregnant, I
> was going through the stage where you want to be a
> mother and keep house. I think Alex was going through
> the same stage. We discussed it and thought it would be
> neat if we had a child, if we got married, all that.

But Alex got in trouble and was sent away to camp early
in Londa's pregnancy. She kept her dreams for awhile.
Alex sent her one letter in which he wrote about his
excitement over the coming baby. When she visited him at
camp two months later, however, Alex told her they
should release the baby for adoption. He said he couldn't
support them. Londa said:

> I was seven months pregnant and that was the first time
> I'd seen Alex in five months. To hear he didn't want the
> baby now...But I had prayed about it before I saw him,
> and that if it was God's will to give the baby up for
> adoption, to have Alex recommend it. And he did, so I
> said, "OK, Lord."
> I learned later that Alex's pastor had talked to him right
> before I saw him. He asked him what kind of a father
> would he make where he was? How could he support it?
> He told Alex the baby would screw up our lives, and Alex
> felt really bad after that. So he told me maybe we should
> give it up.

For each of these young women, the pregnancy at first
appeared to be a reason for rushing an already planned
wedding. She was in love, she wanted to have this baby.
She expected the parenting to be a shared effort. But her
dreams are gone.

No Choice But Adoption

The birthmother may feel she has no choice except
adoption. Perhaps her parents have told her she can't

come home with the baby and she has no place else to go.
Or perhaps she wants a better life for her baby than she
can give him right now.

Julie Vetica, teacher of the School Age Mother program
in La Mirada, California, stresses the importance of
birthmothers making their own decisions about adoption
plans. "If she feels she's pushed into releasing her child, if
she doesn't 'own' the adoption plan, she's likely to become
pregnant again soon after the delivery of this baby," she
observed.

If the birthmother develops an adoption plan and carries
it out, she, who recently lost her boyfriend, will now lose
her baby. She, of all people, needs tender loving care,
needs to be treated with the greatest sensitivity.

Whether she considers an adoption plan through a
licensed agency or with an independent adoption service,
the birthmother needs a counselor who is warm,
empathetic, caring, and who respects her as a person. Too
often the birthmothers interviewed mentioned going to an
agency or to the county for adoption help, then leaving
because they considered the caseworkers cold and
uncaring. Others mentioned similar experiences with
lawyers. It was the face-to-face contact with the helping
person that was most important.

Stephanie, who shared her story in the last chapter,
related her discouraging efforts at finding an empathetic
counselor:

> First my mom called an adoption agency. The counselor
> came out to our house, but she made it all sound so
> complicated. She said I had to find the father, that I had to
> hunt him down. That's their responsibility. He was the last
> person I wanted to see.
>
> We would have to pay all the hospital expenses. She
> made it seem like they just wanted my kid, they didn't
> want the bills, they didn't want to know me. They wanted
> the baby.
>
> I even saw an attorney. That was a bummer. When I
> walked in his office, he looked like he was ready to go

play golf. He pulled out a big tablet and said, "So you want the parents to have a big backyard?" Then he said, "I know a family — they make good money and they could pay you $10,000." Then he started asking me all kinds of stupid questions like the one about the backyard, whether or not they had a dog — nothing about their ability to parent my baby. I felt like I was in the twilight zone with him.

Then a friend gave me Claire's phone number at Calvary Chapel. I called and she came right over. She really does care. I went with her a few times to visit some other girls in the hospital who were pregnant. She went out of her way to show them support and love. She works with maybe fifteen girls at a time, but she was there whenever I needed her. I would call her late at night and she was there.

A birthparent planning an adoption is likely to be emotionally upset. She may feel totally powerless. Her boyfriend splits, her parents say she can't come home with the baby. The last thing she needs, when she finally has the courage to call about adoption, is to be greeted more coldly than if she were buying a dress for the senior prom.

She needs someone who hears her hurt, and who is there to help her work our her plans to make as good an adoption as possible for herself and her baby.

Arlana — Alone and Bitter

Arlana didn't feel any effort was made to meet her needs. Juan suddenly decided he didn't want to be a father, didn't want to be married, when she was five months pregnant. After two months of agonizing indecision, she decided adoption might be the only answer.

She went to an agency in her home town. She says she was told she could look at profiles of available families, but she never received any. She is bitter about the whole situation. As she talked, there were tears in her eyes.

If I had it to do over, I would choose the family. The agency made all these promises and they didn't come through. They said it was all because I delivered early. They promised me pictures, lots of pictures, and all they sent was five. They (the adoptive couple) can't even write me a thank-you letter. I write a thank-you for a birthday card. I give them my baby and there's not even a thank-you.

I could write them but what's the point? I gave them something, they need to write to me first. I finally got my baby in my arms, and the social worker calls up. It's like the baby wasn't mine even for a minute.

I have this baby out in the world someplace and you know, I love that baby. If I didn't love her, I wouldn't have placed her for adoption. If you love someone, you want her to have the best life possible and that's what I did.

My family doesn't even talk about it. They are divorced and I live with my mother.

Even the hospital hassled me. First of all, my baby had a temperature problem so she was under the heat lamp for quite a while. Then they told me I could walk down to where she was and hold her. But I said I wanted to see her there in my room. At first they wouldn't do it, so I told them I hadn't given her up yet. Five minutes later they brought her in.

Then I went down to the nursery where all the other babies had their names on the cribs. All mine had was a big blue card with the agency symbol on it and a sign, "Do not announce." I went home Saturday morning and she was placed a week later. I signed the papers after I left the hospital. I got the five pictures when she was a month old.

They didn't want to give me her wristband but I finally got it after pushing long enough. I've carried it in my wallet ever since.

I wrote her a letter but I never mailed it. What's the point? The agency screens the letter and says you can't say this and you can't say that.

It's hard. It's like everything I ever loved I've lost.

Arlana feels especially forlorn because she can't share her feelings with her baby's adoptive parents. Since she's not in contact at all, there's not much she can do except be bitter, a rough situation for a 16-year-old. Hopefully, she can return to the agency for some much-needed post-placement counseling.

Stress on Both Sides

Amy is another young birthmother who lost her dreams:

> I was happy when I found out I was pregnant. I was with the baby's father for the first five months and I thought we'd get married. He kept telling me I shouldn't give the baby up for adoption, that we would get married in a few months. Instead he cheated on me and finally left me.
>
> He's in Texas somewhere. I told him I was giving the baby up and he said, "No, you're not. I'm coming down there and get my baby." He's never been back.
>
> I live with my dad and there are a lot of problems. He said I'd have to find someplace else to live if I kept the baby. Dad's girlfriend took me down to check on welfare but she told me how hard that would be.

Amy's adoptive parents need to be super sensitive to her situation. Luckily, before Mike and Tricia adopted Amy's baby, they attended an all-day seminar which included a good discussion of birthparents' needs. They understand how hard it was for Amy to release her baby to them.

They are especially concerned because Amy didn't receive much counseling. She came to the adoption service a week before she delivered her baby. She chose Mike and Tricia on Wednesday, met them over lunch Sunday, and gave birth to Kelly the next day. Two days later Kelly was with Mike and Tricia, and Amy returned to her father. He had told her she absolutely could not bring the baby home and he didn't want to talk about it.

But Tricia and Mike also were feeling a lot of stress. Three days before they learned that Amy had chosen

them, they discovered Tricia was pregnant — after trying
for years with no success. They almost said they didn't
want Amy's baby. They decided to go through with it
because Amy, when she heard the news, said that it made
no difference. She still wanted them to adopt her baby.

Two weeks after she was born, Kelly developed a
medical problem which required emergency surgery. Three
days later, Tricia miscarried. Of course Mike and Tricia
were delighted they had adopted Kelly, whose surgery had
corrected her problem. However, their emotions, along
with Amy's, were riding a roller coaster by this time.

Meeting each other's needs is a big task for Amy, Mike
and Tricia. Sometimes when Amy gets especially
depressed, she wonders why Mike and Tricia don't write
more often, why they don't send more pictures. In this
mood, she has written two or three letters asking these
questions, rather negative questions in Mike and Tricia's
viewpoint. Amy is disappointed when she doesn't hear
from them for three or four weeks. She's depressed. Her
baby is gone. She needs cheering up.

Mike and Tricia's feelings are hurt by the letters. They
made a video in the hospital of Amy and Kelly and sent
Amy a copy. They've sent other pictures. They know they
have done more for her than many people would do. In
fact, friends who adopted a child and have no contact
with the birthmother wonder why they do so much.

"In the last letter she called Kelly 'my baby,' " Tricia
reported. "Amy gave birth to her and she still senses she
is hers. I don't mind answering her letters, but I get upset
when I get one and it takes me two weeks to cool down."

Amy even wrote them once and asked what they would
do if she demanded her baby back. She said later that if
Tricia and Mike had responded in anger, had accused her
of having no feelings, of being selfish, she might have
indeed taken the baby back.

Instead, Tricia was strong enough and wise enough to
write, "We would be devastated if we lost Kelly, but until
the adoption is final, she is yours. If you decided to take

her back, we would have to accept it. We both pray that
you don't."

In this adoption triangle, as in most, stress runs
rampant. But because Amy, Tricia and Mike all care about
Kelly and are putting her welfare above their own feelings,
it's working. Because Amy doesn't want to hurt Tricia and
Mike, and because Tricia and Mike care and are concerned
about Amy, it's working. And especially because there's an
understanding counselor acting as an intermediary when
needed, it's working.

Amy's Pregnancy

This is Kelly's story, and it begins with Amy's pregnancy:

First I called an agency, but they said they would put my
baby in foster care at first, and I didn't want that. They let
me pick out a family and I went out to lunch with the
mother. But I didn't like her — she was the snooty type. I
said I wanted pictures and she said no. I asked if I could
see him later and she said no.

So I called Claire. By this time I was more than eight
months pregnant. She showed me a bunch of descriptions
and I picked out Tricia and Mike. Tricia, Mike and I went
out to lunch the next Sunday and I was having
contractions the whole time.

Late that night I was scared and I tried to wake my dad.
I told him I was in labor and he said, "No, you're not,"
and he went back to sleep. I called my mother and she
took me to the hospital.

I had the baby with me the whole time I was in the
hospital. It was real hard. I didn't know how I'd feel. I told
the doctor I didn't want to see the baby, but after I had
Kelly, I wouldn't let them take her away from me. The
doctor said, "You're going to adopt your baby out, so you
can't have her." I said, "You're crazy," and they gave her to
me.

My mom came in and she was mad at me because I had
the baby. I told her this was my way of saying goodbye to
her. She took a lot of pictures for me.

My friend Chondra came to the hospital and brought me a bunch of stuff for the baby. She didn't know I was going to give Kelly up. A couple of months earlier we talked about how I could get on welfare and move in with Chondra and her family. But I couldn't handle that because there are too many people over there.

So when Chondra came to my room I started crying. She wanted to know why I'd do that — adopt Kelly out. I told her that her parents would help her but I didn't have that. So she left.

I have some friends, former friends, who are totally against me for what I did. They go, "How could you give your baby up?" I tried to explain to them that I'm 17, I don't have a job, and I'm not married. They say that's no reason.

I didn't think it would be anything, the adoption, but it was. I thought I'd forget about it right away. Sometimes I regret it and sometimes I don't. I just have to be totally busy or I'll sit here and look at Kelly's pictures and read their letters and get totally depressed.

I went out to lunch with Claire the week after I had the baby. I call her every once in a while and we just talk. If I have a question and don't want to write a letter, I call and ask her.

She didn't try to talk me into the adoption. It had to be my decision. And it really was my decision because of my dad. I'm not going to live out on the street with my baby.

Tricia and Mike's Experience

Tricia and Mike became an important part of Kelly's story. They shared their experiences:

Tricia: Lindsay was born to us, but we couldn't get pregnant again. Finally, after three years, we decided on adoption. Our cousin adopted through the House of Ruth and that's how we got started.

We filled out their forms, then went to their all-day seminar where we learned about open adoption. We also got some insight into how birthparents feel, how hard it is for them when they place a baby for adoption.

Mike: Amy didn't make up her mind about adoption until she was about eight months pregnant. She had been working with another group for a long time but they wouldn't tell her anything about the baby after it was placed, so she came to the House of Ruth. Amy picked us out on a Wednesday and Claire called us that night.

But would you believe that Tricia had discovered she was pregnant the preceding Sunday? Our first thought was to say no to Amy, but when we asked Claire why Amy picked us out, she said it was because our pictures showed us doing all sorts of things — going to Disneyland, visiting my mother in Alaska — Amy wanted her child to be able to lead this kind of life.

Tricia: We decided not to say no right then, but asked Claire to tell Amy we were pregnant. We figured she would want to make another choice. But Amy said that was fine. In fact, Claire said Amy was thrilled for us.

Mike: So that Sunday we took her out to lunch, spent several hours with her, and took lots of pictures. When we left, Amy was having some pain and some bleeding, so we urged her to call her doctor. The next morning at 4 A.M. Claire called to tell us Amy was in labor. Kelly was born that afternoon. We went down that night and had a nice visit with Amy and saw Kelly.

The next day we went down to pick Kelly up. However, the social worker didn't think Amy had made up her mind about the adoption, so she decided to keep her an extra day. We spent several hours with Amy. She's pretty emotional and seems awfully young. She's 17. Then her mom showed up and they talked for a long time. After that, the social worker brought us the papers Amy had signed.

Tricia: We took pictures and made a video of Amy, the baby, and Lindsay. We almost didn't get Lindsay into the room because they said only siblings were allowed. We said Lindsay would soon be a sibling.

The hard part was when we went home. When it was time to leave, Amy had been holding Kelly. I had to take the baby from Amy and that was hard.

Mike: We made copies of the pictures and of the video and sent them to Amy.

She had less time for counseling than most girls have before delivery and I think that made it harder for her. She didn't really know what to expect. She still writes, but a lot of her questions are kind of negative — "You told me you were going to write, you were going to send pictures." Of course we're writing and sending pictures, but apparently not as often as she'd like.

I think we'll have as much contact with Amy as she wants as long as she's rational about it. I don't think it will hurt Kelly because she's going to grow up and say, "Well, she's my birthmother so what's the big deal?"

6

Lutheran Social Service of Texas — Openness with Care

Prominent in the open adoption movement is Lutheran Social Service of Texas. Kathleen Silber, formerly Regional Director, LSST, San Antonio, and co-author of *Dear Birthmother* (1982: Corona), pioneered the practice of open adoption in Texas. This began in 1977 with the initiation of letter and picture exchanges and evolved into face-to-face meetings in 1981.

Janet Cravens-Garner became the Regional Director of the Corpus Christi office of LSST in 1980. Both she and Silber became concerned as they observed adult adoptees and birthparents from the past who were involved in searching. These individuals shared their pain and problems associated with traditional adoption.

This led to a gradual modification of the program at LSST to be more responsive to the needs of all parties, especially the child.

LSST Definition of Open Adoption

By "open adoption," Silber and Cravens-Garner mean any form of communication between adoptive parents and birthparents. They make it clear that open adoption is not shared parenting. Whatever level of openness they choose, the adoptive parents are clearly the psychological parents.

In fact, the birthparents and adoptive parents usually do not meet until after the baby is born and the final adoption decision has been made. The majority do not share fully identifying information at this time, although they may do so if they wish. Many stay in contact over the years either through the agency or directly.

Before the initiation of the face to face meetings, Cravens-Garner remembers going through a period of reevaluation of her profession. One of her observations was that closed adoption did not ever seem the best choice for the birthparent, and rarely so for the adoptive parents. All of these people seemed to have so much pain...

In fact, Cravens-Garner considered changing professions. She decided to stay in adoption work, but with some new resolutions: 1. Workers should never do anything to influence their clients toward adoption; 2. If a client must part with her child, then the agency has an obligation to help her act as responsibly and to be as involved as possible; 3. All clients (adoptive and birthparents) have the ability to self-determine what is best for them; and 4. Cravens-Garner resolved to work for openness in adoption along with Silber.

In practice, according to Cravens-Garner, open adoption means: Birthparents have unlimited access to their child during hospital and foster placement (if foster care is used); they are welcome to exchange letters, pictures, gifts, etc., with the adoptive family; they may meet the adoptive family; and both sets of parents may engage in on-going contact.

"In traditional practice, the social worker holds all the control," Cravens-Garner commented. "She decides who will get the child. She has a God-like role, and I was not comfortable with that. I was (and am) willing to take on the adoption system to make changes. Intermediaries must move toward seeing themselves as contractual, helping people who use their special skills to bring together birthparents and adoptive parents."

Two Sets of Parents

Adoption, as defined in *Dear Birthmother,* is the process of accepting the responsibility for raising a child who has two sets of parents. "Adoption is a lifelong process," Silber reminds us. Adoptive parents will never totally parent the child. Birthparents will remain a part of the child's life whether or not they ever meet.

Both Silber and Cravens-Garner frequently speak on open adoption at conferences across the country as well as offering training sessions for agencies interested in modifying their programs toward more openness.

"Birthparents are very concerned that their children will grow up to hate them," Cravens-Garner commented. "They worry that their children will not realize the adoption decision was a sacrifice on the part of the birthmother. This was why we suggested they write a letter to the baby to explain this.

"We found that birthparents who wrote the letter moved more rapidly through the grief process and were relieved of this fear. In addition, adoptive parents who received these letters felt much more empathetic toward the birthparents. The letter writing was the first real step in opening communication between the birthparents and adoptive parents."

Evolution of Openness

The evolution into openness was a slow one, according to Silber and Cravens-Garner. Early in 1981 the LSST offices in San Antonio and Corpus Christi began offering the option of face-to-face meetings and on-going communication between birthparents and adoptive parents.

"I want to stress the word evolution, because it was a very thoughtful well-planned change in our practice," Cravens-Garner emphasized. "We knew we were moving into uncharted territory and we didn't want to make mistakes that could potentially hurt clients."

Prior to initiating this change, LSST caseworkers spent time learning advantages, pitfalls, and techniques from Catholic Family Services of Green Bay, Wisconsin, who had been providing face-to-face meetings between birthparents and adoptive parents.

They also learned as much as possible about private adoption because openness within private adoption had always been possible to some extent. But they were not trying to pattern after typical independent adoption practices because most often no counseling was involved. Lutheran Social Service realized an increase in counseling services would be needed if more openness was to be offered.

Silber explained, "When we started this, it was for the benefit of the child. We felt the child had a lot of questions which were not being answered in closed adoption. Through meeting, the adoptive parents could answer more of the child's questions. We didn't see then the benefits for the adoptive parents and the birthparents.

"Traditionally, adoptive parents have had a lot of fear about the birthmother. Once they love their baby, they cannot understand how she could give up her baby. They fear she will turn up on their doorstep and want the baby.

"Of all our open adoptions, no one has expressed fear about this. The fear of the unknown birthmother can be overwhelming. She is an unknown, but once they meet her, they can drop that fear. For birthparents, we also see benefits. They seem more at peace with their decision, and they may have an easier process of grieving. They will still grieve, of course, but they may be able to cope better," Silber concluded.

Cravens-Garner stressed the absolute necessity of post-placement counseling. She feels this is even more important than working with birthparents while they are pregnant. "We work with birthparents on acknowledging their feelings and their contribution to this child's life," she said.

Extensive Counseling For Adoptive Parents

Couples who wish to adopt a child through LSST pay a $7400 fee (1986), according to Cravens-Garner. They undergo extensive counseling before a child is placed with them.

Adoptive parents in groups of four or five couples must participate in three four-hour seminars with two facilitators during the homestudy process. This is a sharing time, a time when the couples can start exploring how they feel.

During the first session, the topic is birthparents—how they feel, what they say, why they don't have abortions. The presentation always includes a panel of birthmothers including some who released recently and some who released as long as 20 years ago.

The adoptive parents are given reading assignments including *Dear Birthmother,* an excellent book which explains why LSST decided to offer open adoption and how they developed this service. Most important, the book gives a good overview of the feelings of birthparents and adoptive parents through the use of letters written by these individuals to one another.

Would-be adoptive parents are also asked to read other books dealing with infertility and with adoptees searching for their birthparents and birthparents looking for their birthchildren. One of the seminars includes a panel of adoptive parents. During part of this meeting, the facilitators leave the room so the group can talk freely.

The third seminar deals with the child's development and how to talk to one's child about adoption. Emphasis is on the concept that adoption is a life-long experience for all parties involved.

Adoptive parents write their own social histories. "Some social workers don't like this," Cravens-Garner pointed out. "She may say, 'I have people who can't write, who can't express themselves, and they will never be chosen although they are fine people.' In my experience, this is no problem. The adoptive parents are given back a little control over their lives when they can decide what goes in that letter."

In their social history, the adoptive couple specifies how much openness they want with the birthparents. The birthmother has this information when she chooses her adoptive parents.

All of the options are offered in the context of a counseling relationship, Cravens-Garner stressed. "No one walks in the door and is sent into the next room to meet the other people," she said. About 25 percent of the adoptive parents share identifying information on their own. The other 75 percent share through the agency without using last names or addresses.

Birthmother Selects Adoptive Parents

A birthmother who is considering adoption is welcome, generally later in pregnancy, to look at social histories, take them home, and perhaps share with her family or boyfriend. From these she makes a decision. If she wants a face-to-face meeting, this usually occurs after the decision is made and after the baby is born. Most often, this happens the day of placement, and the birthmother may actually hand the baby over to the adoptive parents.

Pat Dornan, Coordinator, Adoption Awareness Center, LSST, San Antonio, explained, "After the birth, she is asked once again to reassess all the elements of making a decision. If she says again that adoption is what she wants, she meets the family and generally she hands her baby to them. While she is in the hospital, she spends as much time with her baby as anyone else. It's a miraculous love time they would not exchange for anything in the world.

"We have women coming to us saying they would never consider adoption if it had to be closed. Open adoption is not the cure-all — but it stops the terrible slamming of the door which has occurred in the past," Dornan added.

Because of the great amount of pressure felt by both sides, a social worker meets with each group before the joint meeting and again afterward. However, when the birthparent(s) and the adoptive parents meet, the worker does not stay with them. The pre-meeting counseling session helps prepare the birthmother and the adoptive parents for meeting. The session afterward is for "debriefing" — to help each individual discuss and evaluate his/her feelings regarding this contact.

When Cravens-Garner talks about open adoption as practiced by LSST, people often ask "what if" questions. What if the birthmother doesn't like the adoptive parents? What if they don't like her? What if she decides not to let them have the baby? What if they don't send the pictures they promised her? "That almost never happens, but if it does, we treat it as a counseling issue. We provide support for exploring their reasons for those reactions," she replies.

By spring, 1986, LSST had facilitated more than 300 adoptions which included face-to-face meetings. A great many more have included some contact. About 70 percent of their clients want all the openness options. This leaves about 30 percent of the birthparents who don't want to meet the adoptive parents but who may engage in other options of open adoption.

About 25 percent of the open adoption families are making the decision to share full names and addresses. "We suggest to people that they wait until they have had a chance to meet several times and have built some trust. If that's their decision, then I want to help them with it. My opinion is that it is a decision which suits some families and birthparents and doesn't suit others," Cravens-Garner commented.

About two-thirds of these families and birthparents continue their correspondence past the first year. About half continue meeting in the second year, but after that they often start pulling back, according to Cravens-Garner. "I'm smart enough not to have a strong opinion about that," she remarked. "I believe people have the right to determine what suits their family. If I see something they don't, I share it, but they have the right to decide."

Birthfathers are included in the counseling whenever possible. They have the same options the birthmothers do in selecting the families, meeting the parents, continuing communication. Although it is a small percentage who are involved, there have been many initial meetings where the birthparents together handed the baby to the adoptive family.

Sometimes the father comes back two or three years later and says he would like to know more about his child. Birthfathers are encouraged to participate in whatever degree of openness they want.

Lorena Chooses Open Adoption

Four years ago Lorena placed her child through Lutheran Social Service of Texas. About two years ago she shared her story:

My child is two years old. Before Jennifer was born it was very important for me to know where she was, that she would not be with strangers, that she would not be gone forever. Meeting Curtis and Lucia at the time was a way to relate to them, to know what they were like, how they felt. It helped me know how she was going to be raised.

When I was looking at options, I didn't realize I could participate in selecting the parents. I remember saying to another social worker, "I don't have to be best friends with them, but I want to meet them, I want to put faces on them." That's how it came about.

The first time I met Curtis and Lucia was when Jennifer was five days old, and it was a real emotional meeting. I guess it didn't really go anywhere because there were too many tears.

We talked about openness, about sharing pictures and corresponding. I shared with them what the contact might mean to Jennifer, that I could know something about her as she grew up.

The first time I got pictures it was emotional, but not in the sense of other birthparents I've talked with who got nothing. I can feel their loss, their tremendous loss. The contact has helped me grow with my decision, know I made the right decision, and get on with my life.

The first pictures they sent me showed only Jennifer. I kept looking and saying, "There must be parents here somewhere." I mentioned it to my social worker and she told them. Now I get pictures of all three. After those pictures I knew, no, I don't want her back. I couldn't even think of stepping in and trying to take her back. That's her family and that's where she is. I love her and I dearly love getting the pictures and the letters. But I'm a birthmother, an important birthmother, and Curtis and Lucia are her parents, biological or not.

I saw them again a few months ago in El Paso where they live. Because of that meeting, I have no fears any more. I know she's normal, I know she doesn't have 11 toes. They were family. I had wondered if she was an outsider, hadn't really been accepted. But they were a family and that was so special for me, to be able to see that. I knew then that what I did was right.

In that second meeting I got to see Jennifer in her sunsuit and sandles, and I was amazed at her curly hair, so much like mine. Because Lucia and I had been corresponding, we knew about each other. We could talk and ask questions because we have grown to love each other. There was a sense of everything being the way it's supposed to be.

In fact, after Phil Donahue focused on TV on some bad situations in open adoption, I got nervous that they were feeling nervous, so I wrote to them that I didn't want Jennifer back, that there is a lot of joy in knowing she is where she is. If I didn't focus on that joy, I would be a basketcase.

I feel that open adoption takes away a lot of the guilt and the anger you feel. I had a lot of anger inside because I didn't know whether what I was doing was really right. There's a lot of guilt tied to adoption, too, because people don't see how you could do this. But I met Curtis and Lucia and I could see it was right. I didn't have to feel guilty because I got pregnant when I wasn't supposed to. I gave somebody a gift and they have all this love.

My adoptive parents are very open. I get pictures every two or three months, and they don't feel nervous about sharing things with me. I feel part of it, part of my child's life. Being a birthparent isn't easy, and I'm sure it's harder if you're closed off and you never know. There are a lot of worries — you lie awake at night and you worry. Is she all right? But seeing pictures and knowing the adoptive parents help you know your child is OK and that you're OK.

You don't feel OK, for a long time you don't. You feel like a part of you has been ripped away and there is a big hole and you wonder if it will ever be filled. Seeing that the adoptive parents love you and that you aren't an ogre, somebody whose child is told, "Your mother was an awful person, she didn't want you." I don't think that's true of any birthparent, but in my daughter's case, she will *know* I loved her, that I did the best I could.

After that second meeting, I felt so much better about my life that I lost 35 pounds and decided to go on to college. I want to be a social worker, and I want to specialize in adoption. I think the meeting gave me a lot of momentum to get on with it.

We plan to continue meeting throughout her life. I'll be there if there are any questions. Mostly we just plan to keep in touch.

Jennifer's Family

Curtis and Lucia are ecstatic about adopting Jennifer. They are also extremely positive about the help they received from LSST and about the wonders of open adoption:

It was a real serendipitous thing — I have to believe there was some plan for me to do that. We applied kind of like you do for a mortgage to every agency in the vicinity. Our application was very naive and we assumed that an adoption agency was an agency. We didn't realize there would be overriding philosophies that would impinge on how we felt about adoption. We were one of seven out of 175 families chosen at the March intake.

Counseling was critical to our decision. We were exposed to literature about the adoption triangle and we became sensitive to issues of birthparents and adoptees. Before that, if you had asked me who was in the adoption triangle, I would have said the agency, the adoptee, and the adoptive parents. I don't think I had a lot of biases, it was just an unresolved issue. I guess Pannor's book, *The Adoption Triangle* (1978: Anchor Press/Doubleday), and meeting birthparents face to face were the critical factors in our decision toward open adoption.

My husband and I became real aware of the grief birthparents experience. There was somehow a sense of relatedness. I came to the place where, if I denied my child's birthparents, I denied part of my child. I wanted my child to have unconditional love. I wasn't going to put a condition on my love for her.

Now I will have to be honest and say my husband was reluctant at first, and we have veto power in our family so I didn't agitate — I was just real still about it. The primary goal for me was to parent and to parent well. I would do it the best I could in the situation in which I found myself.

Sure enough, two weeks later he just erupted with the decision that he was prepared to participate in open adoption. I guess I will never know what got him there, but of course I was real available to that. We rewrote our social history and modified it to include openness as an option.

We first applied to the agency in March, and in the beginning of December we decided open adoption was for us. Lutheran Social Services requires a series of interviews, seminar attendance, barrage of papers, testimonials from relatives and friends, and we had to read these books. This was to help us understand adoption and to prepare for our role as parents of an adopted child. The agency is real upfront about the difference between parenting a birthchild and parenting an adoptive child.

When I got to the place where I could visualize myself as an adoptive parent, open adoption made sense. As I could come to terms with my own infertility, open adoption made sense. It was being able to empathize with the birthparent that made a difference for me.

About two months later the process was finalized and we were accepted. Then we were waiting for a baby. We engaged in a lot of magical things — it was important to us not to discuss our acceptance with other people. We got the nursery fairly ready but not completely because that might delay. I guess since I had been infertile for so long it was just one more reminder of how out of control I was to have an empty room for someone not yet available.

Finally in November we got a phone call from the agency indicating that a baby girl was ready for us to adopt in Dallas. The birthmom wanted to meet us so we drove to Dallas with heart in hand. I think I was more scared of the traffic than I was the birthmother!

We met Lorena and her mother. My husband, who is a real stoic German boy, broke down and cried at the end of the interview and told Lorena she should never be ashamed of her adoption decision, and that we will always speak well of her to her child.

We took Jennifer home the next day. I write reams to Lorena — very long letters. At first I sent them through the agency, but not any more. Now we send them directly to each other. I try to send a copy to the agency for their files.

I usually debrief after I talk with her on the phone — debrief means to update the agency and let my social worker hear any issues I might not have heard in the conversation.

Our exchange of last names happened 18 months later when we had our second meeting. After about five letters, Lorena called our social worker and asked for a second meeting. We sent her plane tickets and she spent a day with us and Jennifer.

I think that second meeting really impacted her. I think up until that time she had real grief and had been pretty unsure of what she wanted to do with her life. She was involved with a man who didn't want her to continue her relationship with us. In fact, once he tore up one of our letters. Later she decided our relationship was more important to her than he was.

So after the second meeting, Lorena decided to go on to college and work in the field of social work, specifically adoption. She has moved out of her parents' home and really wants to become an educator. I think it gave her a lot of momentum and acceptance.

I worry that open adoption may become a marketing tool rather than an overriding philosophy of commitment to birthparents. I advocate open adoption as LSST practices it.

Post Script

The above interviews occurred two years ago. Recently Lorena and Lucia each called me. They still live 400 miles apart, but they continue to see each other twice a year. Lucia described one of these meetings:

Jennifer enjoys Lorena's visits more and more. When she was three we visited Lorena's home. The first thing we saw was a collage of photos, pictures of Jennifer's birth and many others we had shared.

Jennifer looked at them, then said matter of factly, "That's right, you're my birthmom. I came out of your womb but this is my mom now." I saw an expression of pain on Lorena's face, and then it changed to something like relief. I think she is comfortable with the adoption decision.

Lorena talked about a more recent visit:

Two months ago I went to Jennifer's first dance recital. She was the cutest bumblebee there.

We keep in touch regularly, and it's gotten easier. The feeling of something missing is starting to subside, but I don't think it will ever completely go away.

The more I see them, the more I see her growing up, maturing, somehow it doesn't hurt as much. Being around and watching them grow as a family means a lot to me. To see her worship the ground her daddy walks on is very special.

She knows she has two mothers and we both love her very much. She understands very well, considering her age. She says I'm her birthday mom — I gave her a birthday.

7

Preventing Disrupted Adoption Through Counseling

Mention open adoption and someone inevitably brings up the latest thriller on TV about the troubled teenage birthmother who tries to get her baby away from those loving adoptive parents. Or someone tells about the neighbor all set to adopt a baby and "that girl changed her mind."

Victorie McEvoy, former Outreach Coordinator for the Independent Adoption Center, Pleasant Hill, California, said a lot of people worry that in open adoption the birthparent will come back for her child. "That's a myth for two reasons," she explained. "First of all, whether or not it is an agency or independent adoption, open or closed, it must be approved by the state before it's finalized. But once it's finalized, the birthparent no longer has any legal rights. So she cannot come back and get the child.

"The second myth is that she will want to come back and get the child. From what we know, it's the direct opposite. When she knows where the child is and she's living with the reality, she is much more at peace with the decision she has made."

Laws vary from state to state, but as Victorie said, in independent adoption there is a waiting period between the time the child is placed with the adoptive parents and the point at which s/he becomes legally their child. While it is not common, it is possible for the birthparent to change her mind and get her baby back at any time until she signs the final papers.

Of course it would be a terrible blow to have a baby in one's home for three months and then have that baby taken away...or to have the baby for even a week. It is also a big disappointment to expect to have a baby at a certain time, then be informed that baby is staying with his birthparents.

Intensive Counseling for Adoptive and Birthparents

People seem more likely to be concerned about the adoptive parents' feelings than about the birthparents. But grief is grief, whether you're a birthparent or an adoptive parent. It hurts to lose a baby, and in adoption, *somebody loses*. That can't be prevented, although counseling can help clients deal with their grief.

The best way to minimize the grief of adoptive parents who lose "their" baby, whether before or after placement, is to provide top-notch pre- and post-adoption counseling for both the birthparents and adoptive parents. This can help the adoptive parents realize the possibility of not getting the expected child. Good counseling should also help birthparents make a more firm decision before birth. If they decide to keep, that decision is made before the adoptive parents have been told about the coming baby.

Nearly every professional and many of the birthparents and adoptive parents interviewed for this book emphasized the need for counseling. Donna says later in this chapter, after "losing" two babies to their birthmothers, that she and Ted made sure the third birthmother was deeply involved in counseling before she made her final decision to release her child. Others who wanted open adoption mentioned choosing either an independent adoption service or an agency offering open adoption. They did not simply call a lawyer because they wanted to be assured the birthparents would receive adequate counseling.

A lawyer will perform the legal services required for an adoption. However, the birthparents are generally on their own in sorting out their feelings and coping with the inescapable grief they experience if they release their child.

Grief Counseling

An adoption attorney once said to me, "My birthmother clients don't need counseling. They know what they want to do or they wouldn't be here."

People who consider birthparents their primary clients know better. Janet Cravens-Garner, Lutheran Social Service of Texas, emphasizes that the birthparent needs first of all to know her rights. She needs constant help in grappling with her feelings because she may be deeply into denial. She is likely to cling to that denial as long as possible because the idea of carrying a child for nine months, then parting with it, is too hard.

"There's nothing a potential birthmother needs more than unbiased counseling before her baby's birth and even more after she releases," commented Cravens-Garner. "She needs lots of help in dealing with her grief. She needs to learn about the stages of grief. Ideally, she will work through some of her grief before her baby is born.

"You want your clients to make a responsible decision, so you have to tell them to talk about the long-term implications — there will be days when they regret it," continued Cravens-Garner. "They are birthparents from now on. Mother's Day and birthdays will be tough. She will never be the nurturing parent and she will probably think about her baby often."

Importance of After-Birth Decision

After the baby's birth, she needs permission to redecide, and she needs assurance that this is her right. Some counselors recommend she put her child in foster care for a week while she makes her final decision. Helen Magee of Options for Pregnancy Through Adoption, Seattle, Washington, says some of their clients take their babies home from the hospital for a few days, then release. This gives them a chance to say goodbye.

But won't this make her change her mind? Won't she keep her baby if she cares for him for a few days? Wasn't it easier for her in the "old" days when she didn't even see her baby?

It is true that some young mothers planning adoption decide, when their newborn is laid in their arms, to keep their babies to rear themselves. But this may be a good decision for them. Many birthparents who released without ever seeing their babies spent years regretting their decision.

It's important to help other people in the birthparent's life understand the intense sadness she will feel after her baby is placed. People around her may panic and think she must be making the wrong decision. Or she may change her mind because she had no idea how much it would hurt to release her baby. Anything that hurts that much must be wrong. She needs to know that something can hurt a lot and still be right.

It's extremely important to separate the adoption issue from the choice of family. In open adoption, this may present a dilemma. By law, she can't make her final decision about adoption until after the birth of her baby. Yet for many, the family is chosen, the parties meet, and may spend time together for several months before the birth. For some birthparents, this is a workable and very reassuring plan.

If she is firm in her adoption decision, fine. Forming a relationship with the adoptive parents before the baby is delivered can be a beautiful experience for everyone. Adoptive parents have memories to share with their child. The birthmother may grieve for a shorter time because she is confident she has chosen the right parents for her baby.

But there are two risks in this situation. First, even if the birthmother and the adoptive parents bond together before delivery, she may still decide to keep her baby. If she does, the adoptive parents may be more devastated than if they had been waiting for a baby whose mother is a stranger.

The other, and perhaps more important, risk is that the birthmother may feel pressured to release her baby because of the relationship she has already established with the birthparents. How can she possibly change her mind and disappoint this couple she has grown to love? Irene, whose story follows, was especially concerned because the adoptive parents had eaten at her family's table. Other birthparents interviewed for this book commented that they would not have changed their minds because of the bonding with the adoptive parents. "If I had kept him, they would have been heart-broken."

This is why Lutheran Social Service of Texas and some other agencies prefer that their clients not choose the adoptive family, or at least not have a face-to-face meeting, until after delivery and after the final decision to release is made. Other adoption services feel strongly that the pre-birth bonding process is important. The best answer probably lies within each client. Each approach is best for some, but not for all.

But what if she does change her mind and decide to parent her baby? Most of the counselors said they stress over and over with adoptive parents that this may happen. It's not likely to happen after placement but, especially in independent adoption, it is a possibility.

Agencies and adoption services offering some form of open adoption usually expect would-be adoptive parents to attend an all-day seminar, support group meetings, and/or counseling sessions. Almost always birthparents are an important part of these meetings.

Often a couple is so immersed in their own infertility problems that they cannot see beyond the baby in their adoption plans. They need to understand that birthparents are real people who think about, plan for, and love their babies. Generally the birthparents place their babies' needs above their own or they would not be considering adoption.

Adoption workers stress that offering open adoption takes a great deal more time on their part. "We don't just throw people together and hope it works," one commented.

A carefully planned adoption decision firmly made by the birthparents and reconfirmed after the baby's birth is not likely to be changed. With open adoption, the decision may be more firm because the birthparents will not lose all contact with the baby if they decide to place him. This usually is very comforting to them.

Adoptive Parents Sometimes "Disrupt"

Perhaps the term "disrupted adoption plan" should be applied to a different situation. Several birthmothers in this book mentioned planning an adoption with a couple who then backed out of the arrangement. Pati in chapter 12 talks about interviewing six couples and choosing one to parent her baby. She developed a good relationship with the adoptive mother who, to Pati's consternation, adopted another baby not long before Pati's delivery date. For the same reason, Jayne (chapter 14) also had to choose another couple to parent her child.

DeeDee and Rick in chapter 8 developed a relationship with Denise while Denise was pregnant. A month before Denise's baby was due, DeeDee and Rick were offered a baby through the county adoption service. They declined because of their commitment to Denise. As they point out, trust and commitment go both ways.

Birthmother Stresses Counseling

After her son had been with his adoptive parents for three weeks, Irene decided she would rear him herself. If she had had counseling, she feels she probably would have kept him from birth. She realizes now that making a firm decision before placement would have prevented at least some of the grief the adoptive parents had to endure.

I had one session of counseling before Chris was born and I didn't like that counselor. I convinced myself I didn't need it. I'm sorry now because if I'd had more and better counseling, I wouldn't have let him go in the first place. I'm sorry Chris wasn't with me those first three weeks, and I'm also sorry to have hurt Bob and Mickey.

I give a lot of credit to girls who can go through with adoption. It takes a lot of strength, and you have to be totally unselfish. But I think it's important they get a lot of counseling,, and that they be real sure in their decision. They need to think about it a lot. They shouldn't just say, "I'm not going to think about it." That's what I was doing. Then when the baby comes, it's super hard to face what's happening.

Biological Parenting Offers No Guarantee

There is no guarantee that a closed adoption will be permanent. As a matter of fact, biological parenting comes with no guarantee. About 20 percent of all pregnancies end in miscarriage. Some babies are stillborn, and others die within the first year. Whether adoptive or biological, parenting does not start with a gift tied with a blue (or pink) ribbon accompanied by its own guarantee.

The best way to avoid broken adoptions is to prevent placement of babies whose birthparents are not sufficiently sure of their adoption plan. Too often, in independent adoption the birthparent approaches an attorney or tells a neighbor she might release the baby.

The neighbor or the attorney knows this couple looking for a baby. They bring the parties together whether or not they actually meet each other face-to-face. The birthparent has no help in dealing with her decision. She may be sure she cannot rear this child herself, so she expects releasing him to be no big deal.

But when the baby is born, she discovers she has very strong feelings. This is her baby and already, to her surprise, she experiences amazing love for him. At this point she may change her mind and decide she can somehow parent this child.

Irene's Story

Or she may do as Irene did. Irene, a short, dark-haired, bright young woman, became pregnant late in her junior year of high school. Her family didn't like her boyfriend although she continued to see him. Her mother encouraged her to consider adoption.

She talked to a lawyer about adoption. She didn't think she needed counseling, and thought she'd release her baby because that's what everyone seemed to expect:

My mom pushed adoption right away. She'd say. "There's no way you and Ed can do this. You're too young, you need to grow up."

Finally Ed and I called a lawyer my mom knew. The lawyer said we could talk to the couple and decide if we wanted them to have our baby. But the first two couples we saw backed out. One got another baby after they said they wanted ours, and the other one decided they weren't ready to adopt.

So she introduced us to another couple. We liked them. He's a college professor and she stays home. We talked for almost two hours, and they came over to our house for dinner that night.

Actually I wouldn't advise that. When I changed my mind, it was harder because we had them in our home and they were sitting at our table with us. That just made them more resentful toward us at the end. One meeting is all right, but then I think it would be best to break away unless you're absolutely sure you're going to release your baby.

I saw Chris every day in the hospital. I had a C-section so I stayed for four days. I saw him a lot.

The night after Chris was born was awful. Several of my friends came to visit me and we were making a lot of noise, so we closed the door. Then here came Bob and Mickey barging in. Then the nurse said my friends had to leave because they were bringing the baby in. She let Bob and Mickey stay and they held Chris more than I did.

My friends were still outside the door, and that bothered me a lot — having Bob and Mickey holding Chris as if he was already theirs. That was real hard.

I had him early Monday and went home Thursday. On Wednesday me and Ed started crying a lot and we said our last goodbye in this little room in the hospital. Then they wheeled him away while we watched and it was real hard.

Ed and Irene Reconsider

Then when I got home we started thinking about it more because it's something you can't just not think about. A week later we sat down and talked, and Ed said, "You know we can get him back. It's hard on the adoptive parents, but we can't do this just because of them."

We told my mom and she was real defensive. She said, "You can't do it, you'll wind up hating Chris, and you guys won't be able to stay together."

I told her, "But mom, this is what I have to do." Then I called Mickey and she said Bob would call me back because she couldn't talk right then.

Bob called me and said, "It's not that easy. I have to call my lawyer." I said, "On what grounds?" and he said, "Because I have my son." From that point on he talked through my mom. I never talked to him again.

He called my mom and said his lawyer told him they had a good chance of keeping Chris. She told him, "We talked to lawyers, too, and they say Irene hasn't signed any papers and you have no rights."

Several people told me I wouldn't need a lawyer but I ought to get one just in case. They said the only thing Bob could do was get a guardianship paper from the court and try to prove I was an unfit mother. After that it was a waiting game. Bob said he'd call us back, but he never did.

Because Mom insisted, I finally decided to see a counselor, so we called Sharon Kaplan. (Kaplan is director of Parenting Resources in Santa Ana, California, and co-author of *Cooperative Adoption* [1985: Triadoption Publications].) I spent an hour with her. Sharon was nice and helpful, real understanding, and she didn't take sides. But it was nervewracking because she really tried to help me think through very carefully whether or not I really wanted to parent Chris right now. I'm glad I went.

Then Sharon called Bob and Mickey's lawyer. She told them she thought I was set in my decision and that she thought I'd be a good mom. So he called Bob and Mickey and told them. In the meantime, my lawyer had written them a letter saying legally I had all the rights and could simply go and get Chris.

Then all five of us had a counseling appointment with Sharon. We were sitting in the waiting room while the counselor was getting acquainted with Bob and Mickey. My mom and Ed's mother were there, and so were Mickey's parents. They knew who we were, but they kept talking out loud about how they couldn't understand how anybody could do this. "How could she do such a mean thing?"

Then the counselor called us in with Bob and Mickey and asked us some questions. Mickey got mad at everything I said. I told them I was going to put Chris in daycare while I work. She acted as if nobody else did that. Sharon asked if there were any special toys Chris liked. Mickey was very defensive and said, "You sound like I'm giving him to a babysitter. I don't want to answer that." While they talked, Mickey and Bob were playing with Chris and feeding him.

Then they said, "I know you didn't expect us to bring Chris with us today, but we decided we'd give him to you now because it hurts too much to go on like this."

So they went into the back room and said goodbye to Chris. Then the counselor brought him out to us. Of course that was hard for them.

Two Months Later

I've had Chris for two months now. Two weeks after I got him, Bob wrote my mom a letter — not to me, but to my mom. I can almost remember it because I've read it over and over. He said, "Dear Susan: It has been almost two weeks since we gave up John." They had named him John, and right there it sounds as if they were the ones who gave birth and are releasing him. "I'm writing to you because at this point I don't think Irene could understand how we feel." Then he said I had broken a trust with him and he was sorry our relationship had to end that way.

Bob said I was real immature and that Ed and I didn't have a chance together. My mom asked if I thought she should write back to him. I said only if she wanted to but I didn't see any reason to respond. I can understand Bob's feelings, but if he wanted to say that, he should have said it to me. He said, "Irene can't possibly understand how we feel." Well, I'm the person who can most understand how they feel because I was there.

I told Sharon that if Bob and Mickey ever wanted to see Chris or if they wanted to call to see how he was doing, that would be all right. But they said no, because it would be too hard for them. It is hard because they are feeling exactly as we did, but they're saying I'd never understand those feelings.

I think I agreed to adoption mostly to please my mom. I have always been that way. I have explained it to her, and I think our relationship is changing. She's been real accepting.

I think my biggest mistake was going through a lawyer. I don't think anybody should do that, especially if the lawyer represents both the adoptive and the birthparents. Ours represented both, and she said when one of us changed our mind, she couldn't represent either of us. I suppose I signed that agreement, but when I called the lawyer, it was a big shock to hear her say, "Irene, I can't help you because you changed your mind." I was the one that had called her in the first place.

I'm sorry about the grief we caused Bob and Mickey, but I have absolutely no regrets for keeping Chris. I wish I had never agreed to adoption.

Donna and Ted Try Again

Donna and Ted also had to face the grief of losing a child, in fact, two babies, because their birthparents changed their minds. But they persevered and now have a beautiful daughter. Donna shares their story:

We were married in 1974. I don't work because I was always going to be a mother and this was my career. But I didn't get pregnant month after month, year after year.

We went through years of tests, surgeries. We even tried *in vitro* fertilization in 1983. They retrieved four eggs which didn't fertilize. That was especially disappointing.

We finally agreed it was time to check out adoption.

We met Bruce at the Independent Adoption Center April 2, 1984 — I'll never forget the date. We decided this was it, this was the right thing to do. So we dove in. We wrote our letter, took lots of pictures, and had hundreds of copies made. We sent them to friends, to lists of doctors, to school programs for pregnant teenagers. In July a nice young couple contacted us.

We met them both, and I went down to meet her family. We spent an afternoon together. We talked at least once a week by phone during those two months. Everything was set for us to have our baby.

She delivered in September. We were walking out the door to go to the hospital (floating, you might say) when the telephone rang. They had changed their minds and decided to parent their baby.

That was hard. We'd been trying for ten years to have a baby and once again we'd failed.

But we didn't give up. We kept plugging along, waiting and waiting, and mailing out lots and lots of letters.

Then six months later we got a letter from a friend. She told us about a young lady who was 16 and who felt she absolutely could not parent her baby. We were real excited although we knew she was up and down, changing her mind every few days.

When her baby was born, we flew to San Diego. She didn't want to meet us, but we met her parents. We brought our beautiful little boy home the next day. He had dark hair and was super alert. We named him Rodney. We were so proud of him. In the middle of all the commotion of feeding, caring for, and loving our son, I ecstatically sent out fifty birth announcements.

A week later his birthmother changed her mind. She and her boyfriend came up to our house and took him back. We were devastated. This was much worse than the first time.

How much more could we handle? But we knew we wanted a child. We weren't about to quit.

Then Bruce at the Independent Adoption Center came up with a lead for us. A young lady, Cyndi, had picked us, and again, the birthfather was also involved. They gave

Cyndi lots of counseling, lots of time to think it out. We met her and her boyfriend and we had dinner with them several times.

Dawn was born in May and it all worked out beautifully. She's blonde, blue-eyed, and gorgeous. She was absolutely worth waiting for. It's uncanny that she so resembles both our families.

For awhile Cyndi called twice a week, then every couple of weeks, then every other month. Now we haven't heard from her since she was here for Dawn's birthday three months ago. Cyndi has found a new boyfriend and is getting married in a few weeks.

The first time Cyndi visited us was when Dawn was nine months old. I was real frightened. Then I thought, just before she arrived, "This is silly. There is nothing to be fearful about. The adoption has been final for two months."

Then when I saw Cyndi, it was nice and I had no fear. It was great for her to see that Dawn was OK. She had never seen our house and she wanted to know where her baby was living.

Cyndi also brought her sister and two little nephews who got to meet their cousin. As a matter of fact, Dawn has another "birthcousin" who is also adopted, and I have pictures of him. His adoptive parents know of us, and who knows? We may meet later on.

Our friends were mostly with us during all this time, but a few said, "How can you keep doing it?" But we weren't people who give up. Friends have also asked about expenses but it hasn't been that bad.

With the first one, we paid some expenses, but when she changed her mind, her family reimbursed us. They didn't have to from a legal standpoint, but they felt it was right. For Rodney, we were out our legal fees and airfare to San Diego. All three of the birthmothers had welfare for medical expenses.

Through all these years, I almost think our parents suffered as much or more than we did. I think that after so many years of infertility, you get a little numb.

People who experience these tragedies shouldn't give up. Eventually they'll have their baby.

We think Dawn was meant for us.

8

Independent Adoption Center Stresses Counseling

"Most people think they will be terrified at the hospital, that the birthmother will change her mind. The reality is so often different." As he talked, Bruce Rappaport pointed to a large photo on his office wall showing an adoptive couple, a birthmother, and their baby 20 minutes after delivery. The couple looked ecstatic, the mother a bit tired, and the baby — he didn't appear terribly interested.

"There's a bond between all of them. There is a real relationship that's not always easy but always special. The role of the Adoption Center is to help build that relationship," he explained.

Adoption Service Expands Rapidly

Rappaport is director of the Independent Adoption Center, Pleasant Hill, California. The Center has grown from a staff of one (him), a yearly budget of $20,000, and an average of one adoption every six to eight weeks in 1983 to a staff of 12, a budget of over $300,000, and an average of one or two adoptions per week in 1986.

Former director of a San Francisco infertility clinic, Rappaport started the Independent Adoption Center (IAC) because he wanted to offer a service to birthparents and adoptive couples which would combine the counseling and reliability of licensed adoption agencies with the openness and possible timeliness of independent adoption.

The staff includes three professionally trained and licensed counselors. Sally Watson works primarily with adoptive parents in the early stages of their search for a baby. Candace Kunz and Ellie Fisher work with both the birthparents and the adoptive parents as the adoption progresses.

"Our position is that young people considering adoption deserve a great deal of respect, and that only open adoption makes that possible. The young parents need to have a choice," he said.

"We try to persuade and educate adoptive parents about their future child's birthparents. We put a lot of energy into explaining to people the advantages of open adoption. In open adoption, both adoptive parents and birthparents are in control. We don't try to cram it down their throats, but we do succeed in winning people over."

Most couples who come to the Center are middle-income Caucasians 30-45 years old. Generally they both work and have spent several years in infertility treatment. First, they attend a Saturday morning seminar. If they decide to sign up, they are expected to take advantage of the full variety of support services provided by the Center. They are advised to take an active part in the baby search by sending out at least 500 letters and brochures to doctors, counselors, and friends.

Couples Prepare/Follow Marketing Plan

Watson, program director of the Center, described the marketing plan each adoptive couple is expected to carry out. They must prepare a resume in which they describe themselves, their life-style, their interests, and, as Watson puts it, "make an emotional appeal to the birthmother." This, including a photograph, must all fit on one 8-1/2" x 11" sheet of paper.

Watson reviews the couple's work and, if she doesn't think they are presenting themselves as well as possible, tells them to go home and work on it. "I want it to be honest, but I want them to present well," she said.

The picture is especially important, according to Watson. Sometimes a couple will take 100 shots before they get the "right" one. It needs to be spontaneous and casual, yet show them at their best. She recommends a wedding photographer who can take candid shots which look unposed. "I review all this with them because I want them to get a baby," she explained.

"Sometimes, however, when I work with an adoptive couple, I don't feel quite right about them. Then I talk to Bruce about it. Of course if I felt there was something ethically wrong, we wouldn't accept them. But we don't like to put ourselves in a position where we tell somebody they can't have a baby.

"What will happen is that people who aren't ready to have kids don't continue through the process. First, they have to pay the fees. Then if they do all the things I ask them to do in preparation, they have to be serious about it. If they aren't ready to be parents, they won't do all this. Each couple completes a questionnaire and we get references. If something doesn't look right, we start asking about it.

"Sometimes adoptive parents ask me. 'How much do you screen the birthparents for genetic defects?' I ask, 'Did you check each other on that before you got married?' We have an arrangement with an agency who will take a special child, a child who is handicapped. It has not happened yet."

Financial Costs Clearly Stated

A "Financial Aspects of Independent Adoption" handout is given immediately to interested couples. Medical expenses may be minimal if she is covered by MediCal or her own insurance. If not, of course the adoptive couple pays for her prenatal care, labor and delivery.

The birthmother's living expenses related to the pregnancy may also be minimal, perhaps her maternity clothes. Or the couple may be responsible for her full support for two or three months prior to delivery.

Cost of legal services ranges from $1200 to $3500. The Center offers its own Legal Services Plan as an option.

In addition to these expenses, enrollment in the Center — initial fees, educational materials, and counseling expenses — costs from $1400 to $2000 (1986). This covers educational services including orientation and individual counseling sessions, 300 mailing labels for doctors, counselors, and school nurses, and other materials. The couple is also advised to spend $300-$500 on mailings and personal outreach, possibly on advertising. (Advertising that one wants a baby is not permitted in some states.)

The counseling program includes a "match" appointment for couple and birthmother, five to eight counseling appointments for the couple and five to eight for the birthmother. These services are available to any/all birthmothers with whom the clients work until they have completed a successful adoption.

Typically, total costs for an adoption run between $7000 and $8000 including the Center's fees. There are rare cases where it runs much higher. "If the birthmother already has had a child delivered by C-section, we know this delivery may also be C-section. If so, adoption expenses could total as much as $20,000. The first couple the birthmother chooses may not be able to afford this, and we have to be up-front with her about the expenses," Rappaport explained.

Cooperation Agreement Signed By All

Not only do the adoptive couples sign a contract for services, but they and the birthparents also sign a carefully worded "Independent Adoption Cooperation Agreement." The first sentence reads, "This is not a legally binding document."

"When we first started, we had couples who promised they would stay in contact with the birthparent, then backed out later," Rappaport commented. "So we stepped up the contact, the counseling about the positiveness of maintaining contact. Even if we could have a legally binding contract, it would be impossible to enforce. Staying in touch has to be done on faith, but you can help faith along. Ultimately, it's education that wins.

"Now we find that adoptive couples are as likely to be upset at a break in contact as birthparents are. Sometimes a birthmother comes to us and wants to be in more contact and we try to help. But more often the adoptive parents want to stay in touch. We'll call the birthmother and she may say, 'I really don't want to continue seeing them.' Or the adoptive parents will send a letter and it will be returned marked 'Unknown.' At this point we have to intervene as often to encourage adoptive parents to let go as we do to insist they send pictures to the birthparents."

Would-be adoptive parents are advised that if they pay the birthmother's expenses and she decides to parent her child, they will not be reimbursed. Occasionally a birthmother feels she needs to pay it back, but generally she doesn't have the money. "That will never change," Rappaport pointed out. "It's not going to be possible to get the money back because that would be buying the baby."

If the birthmother says she doesn't know where the father is or she won't name him, she is told this puts the adoption in jeopardy. "If a woman really won't tell us who the father is, we have to treat it as high risk," Rappaport said. "We are at the point where we may turn a birthmother down, although that is very unusual. If we think she is a fraud we won't continue working with her. We'll refer her to an agency.

"Often, however, simply being sensitive to people's needs prevents real problems," Rappaport commented. "One young birthmother didn't tell us the truth about the father, and the man who really was the father came into the hospital demanding to see the baby. The lawyers got all excited, and I said, 'Now wait a minute. Maybe he just needs to save face. Invite him in, but don't bring the baby in at first. Talk about a plan. Maybe he can see his child at four months and eight months.' It worked out, and he signed the adoption papers."

Outreach Considered Crucial

Outreach is an extremely important part of the IAC services. Victorie McEvoy, obviously very sensitive to others' needs, was outreach coordinator for the Center until mid-1986. She reported, "I can't keep up with the requests we get for program speakers."

She spoke of making a presentation to a group of nurse practitioners. Afterward, she received several calls from participants who said people had been asking them about adoption for the first time. This means, according to McEvoy, that they had learned to listen to these requests.

When she attended an American Public Health Association meeting in Washington, D.C., she was the only adoption specialist among 5000 people. "They would say, 'Oh, our population isn't interested in adoption.'" she reported. "We have to help professionals understand that they must talk about adoption in just as positive a light as they do about abortion or keeping. They also need to know the resources for adoption in their communities.

"We get a surprising number of birthmother calls," McEvoy commented. "I'd love to spend more time with them. It means so much to me to let them know they have choices.

"Someone called this morning and asked if we 'make' people meet each other. The technical answer, I guess, is 'Yes,' but in actuality we bring them along through counseling so they will decide they want to meet," McEvoy related.

The Center sets up a Holiday Talkline between Thanksgiving and New Year's. Phones are answered by adoptive parents who respond to calls from people facing the frustration of dealing with the disappointment of wanting to be a family and feeling they are not.

Strong Counseling Program Offered

Watson explained that adoption counseling must be learned on the job. Rappaport started out working with volunteers but soon realized he needed a professionally trained staff. "As professionals, we are taught to recognize it when we are no longer being objective. At that point we get feedback from each other," Watson commented.

Clients are counseled for at least a month, often up to six months, according to Watson. The counseling is adoption-related, and they are careful not to get involved in in-depth therapy in life issues. "If the birthmother is telegraphing problems to us through her behavior, we try to prolong the choosing process," she explained. "If she's sociopathic or a drug abuser, she will move on. People with these problems can't stand not having immediate gratification."

Counseling is essentially structured for birthparent clients. When she calls, a staff member will spend up to an hour talking with her. Information is gathered, but the important thing at that point is to help her feel comfortable. Usually she has already decided on adoption when she calls.

She is invited in to the Center and spends about an hour with the counselor. If she appears ready to move on in her adoption planning, she looks through the resume book. She chooses three or four couples and may meet with them soon after this meeting. Or if she wishes, she may take the resumes home and think about it.

When she's ready, she meets her couple. "The Match Meeting is like the most anxiety-producing blind date you have ever experienced," Watson commented. She and Kunz or Fisher, birthmother counselors, attend this meeting and help the birthparent and the adoptive couple learn more about each other. If they choose to do so, their relationship begins. If there are problem areas, the counselors help bring them out. At this time they start talking about the degree of contact each wants. "Usually they work out an agreement fairly easily," Watson said.

Following this meeting the birthparent and the adoptive couple have individual counseling. There may also be further joint counseling sessions. During the last meeting before birth, they will go over their agreement together. Each has already discussed this important topic with the counselor, and they have talked about it together in their prior meetings. "By the time she gets to the hospital, both she and her adoptive couple are well prepared. There has been a lot of exploration of issues," Watson concluded.

"Our job is to be neutral, to facilitate what is going on. If she starts to grieve, to be upset, we don't panic. This doesn't mean she shouldn't release, it simply means she's starting the inevitable grieving.

"There is a period right after birth when the adoptive couple usually wants to withdraw and bond with the baby," Watson explained. "But the birthmother has been courted for several months, and she may wonder, 'Are they rejecting me? Will I not get any pictures?' That's when it's important that we help her understand the adoptive parents aren't rejecting her — they're bonding with the baby. Then after about three months, she is ready to move on and they are ready for more contact and they will say, 'Where did she go?' "

Denise's Story

Denise is a short dark-haired young woman who lives by herself. She's a waitress in an expensive restaurant in a town outside of San Francisco. She's also attending college working toward an accounting degree. During the early months of her pregnancy she was living with her boyfriend:

As soon as I finished high school I moved out. I'd lived with my parents long enough, and I was madly in love. I got a job and we had this little apartment.

I discovered I was pregnant on my 18th birthday. I thought Doug would be pleased, but he wanted me to have an abortion. I refused, and I thought he understood.

We stayed together another month or two, but we argued more and more.

One night we had a bad fight and he hit me. That was it. I told him to get out, I'd manage on my own. I think he was relieved.

By this time I was six months pregnant and I didn't know what to do. I knew I couldn't handle having a baby by myself. I thought about adoption and decided that was what I'd do. I'm adopted and it's been all right. I knew I couldn't give my baby what it deserved.

I was looking into closed adoption. Then my mom was taking this class that DeeDee was teaching. DeeDee had told her class how much she and Rick wanted a baby and she handed out their letters with their picture on them. My mom told me about it and suggested I call the Independent Adoption Center.

I called and talked to Candace. They sent me a bunch of letters including DeeDee and Rick's. I read them all, but my mom said DeeDee was real nice. I picked them, and when I came home for Christmas, I met them.

We went out to dinner and they took me to their house. I met their little son and they showed me their nursery.

I saw Candace quite a few times. We'd talk, and I went to the birthparent support group several times. While I was there I talked to people who had gone through this, and it made me feel better. It helped prepare me, knowing that I'm not the only one.

About this time Doug came over to see me. We talked a long time and decided not to get back together. He promised to support me in my adoption decision, and he did. He even visited the baby three weeks after he was born.

When I was carrying the baby, I knew he wouldn't be mine. This was something I was doing for someone else. I didn't get too attached — I didn't think about all the things I could do if I had a baby. If I'd thought about that, I might have kept him.

Carl was born two months ago. I came home the day after he was born, but we had a little time together in the hospital. It was sad when I left and watched them take him away.

I've seen them three times since then, but not lately because I've been busy. They send me lots of pictures. I call DeeDee every once in a while and ask how the baby is. I think I've gotten over it, but every now and then I get sad. I know it was the best thing I could do.

I'll continue seeing Carl but not too much. I have to go on with my life.

I never thought I was strong before, but after I did this, I decided I was.

DeeDee and Rick Adopt Again

DeeDee and Rick live in a suburb of San Francisco. DeeDee is an artist, and she taught art in a junior high until they adopted their first son, Jimmy, four years ago. Rick owns a small furniture store six blocks from their home.

They were married seven years and had survived a lot of infertility testing when they adopted Jimmy. DeeDee told their story:

We adopted our first child through an agency, and we know very little about his birthparents. At the time we didn't question it. That was the way things were done. Jimmy was three months old when he came to our home, but he wasn't legally free for several months. We had to become foster parents at that time. Of course that was a risk. You have to take risks. Perhaps that's why open adoption wasn't particularly frightening to us.

We had our application in for another baby from the county, but because we had one child, they said it would be a long wait. Then one day I heard Bruce talking on the radio. I realized he was the same person a friend had talked about — they adopted a baby from the Center a year ago.

I called for information and we went to their orientation meeting. One person in the group was a birthmother and she talked a lot about her experience. That helped us understand what a birthmother goes through when she gives up her baby. She also helped us understand open adoption from her point of view.

It took longer than we expected to get our resume finished, find the right picture, and get the whole thing reproduced. It was a little more expensive to go through the Center than we had expected, so that slowed us down.

Finally we started mailing our resumes out. We used the labels they gave us — doctors and counselors from across the country. I went through my sorority roster and sent them to sorority houses. When I saw a newspaper article about youth ministers working with single mothers, I sent them there. I also took them to the students at the night school class I teach.

That did it...about six months later. One of my students told me her daugher was pregnant. Were we still interested? Of course we were!

We were just in time. Denise had started making other plans for her baby. She didn't think she wanted open adoption because she was afraid to know who we were. I suggested she call the Center and talk to a counselor so she could make an informed decision about open adoption.

She went over and talked to Candace. They gave her a packet of about 50 letters including ours. They didn't know we had sent her there, and we panicked a little. What if she chose someone else? But I wrote another three-page letter and sent it to Denise through her mom, and told her a lot more about us and our home.

Denise came home at Christmas and we made an appointment to meet her at the Center. Since we live in the same town which is pretty far from the Center, we decided to ride in together. We got acquainted during that ride.

After the meeting with the counselor, we all decided this was what we wanted to do. Our first task was to help Denise find a place to live because she had left her apartment and her mother said she couldn't live with them. We found her a place by New Year's.

She also let me be there all through labor and delivery. They called us as soon as she went into labor. Her mom and her sister were there, and it was a little crowded, but I got to see everything and I loved it.

We all spent time with Carl in the hospital. Denise had sad moments, but we could tell her resolve was really strong. She knew she was doing the right thing. She's a very sensitive person and she didn't want to cause us distress, but we knew it was hard for her.

We send a lot of pictures right now, but that will probably slow down. We hope she keeps in touch with us. Friends with an open adoption told us that the relationship gradually diminishes over time. One couple was disappointed because they hadn't heard from the birthmother at Christmas.

We said Denise and the birthfather, her parents and his would be welcome at any time. Each time they call they apologize and say, "We really want to see him but we don't want to intrude." Denise has been here three times, Doug, once, his mom, once, and her folks, twice.

What About the Risk?

Friends asked how we could stand the risk. We say everything in life is risky. If we had had a biological child, there would have been a lot of risk involved. Since we couldn't do that, we took this risk.

There's a lot of risk for the birthmother too. I felt a strong commitment to her. I figured if we expected a commitment from her, we needed to be committed too. In fact, a month before Carl was born, the county called and said they had a baby for us. But we had a commitment to Denise. We're hearing more and more stories about adoptions that didn't go through. She changed her mind or she took the baby back after a week. In every case these are people who went through an attorney and didn't get any counseling. I think that's the great part of the Independent Adoption Center - she got counseling.

If we felt nervous, we could call the counselor too. She had been through this enough to warn us about things that might happen.

For example, she told us about the recent birth where everyone watched the birth, then left to see the baby. In their excitement, they left the birthmother totally alone. We made sure somebody stayed with Denise.

These two months have been wonderful. I'm tired but even that's getting better. Carl is very responsive and absolutely gorgeous. Would you believe he looks like Rick?

9

Open Adoption — What About Problems?

Open adoption may be an idea whose time has come (again), but not everyone agrees it's a good practice. Many adoption agencies across the United States still practice closed adoption where the birthparents and adoptive parents never meet and may not know very much about each other. In some states, agencies are forbidden by law to share identifying information between birthparents and adoptive parents.

In spite of the highly positive attitudes toward open adoption shared in this book, closed/confidential placement of infants in nonrelated families still occurs regularly. A great majority of agency adoptions today are of this type. If you are a potential adoptive parent or a birthparent, you may find few if any resources in your area to help you consider the possibility of open adoption.

Independent adoption is legal in most states. Birthparents who place independently choose the adoptive parents and place their child directly with these parents. Therefore, independent adoption by definition is open. In practice, this is not always the case because an attorney or a doctor may actually choose the adoptive parents and place the baby with them.

Many Infants Placed Independently

Fifty to 80 percent (depending on which source one quotes) of the infants adopted in the United States are placed independently rather than through a licensed agency. Too often, independent adoption is carried out with no counseling provided for anyone. The baby is simply placed with the adoptive couple.

Independent adoption can work well *if* all parties involved are exceptionally mature, caring, rational people — and nothing goes wrong. But not everybody involved in most adoptions is exceptionally mature, caring, and rational, and something *can* go wrong. Independent adoption with no intermediary, while it is "open" adoption, may not serve the best interests of everyone involved.

The three independent adoption services described in this book appear to be reputable, and to be staffed by caring and capable people. Charges for their services vary, but each is apparently operating strictly within the limits of the law. There are similar services in other areas of the United States, but in many communities this kind of help is not available.

Some independent adoption services consider adoptive couples to be their primary clients. In the business world, this makes sense because they are the ones paying the bills. But facilitating adoptions *must* be a human service first. It is absolutely essential that birthparents be treated with respect and sensitivity.

Anyone working with an independent adoption service needs to know as much about that service as possible. They also need to know the laws in their state or province which pertain to adoption.

For areas in which no licensed agency or reputable adoption service is providing open adoption, the birthparents and/or adoptive parents wanting this kind of help may be out of luck. If they choose to go out of state to find either adoptive parents or a baby to adopt, the risk multiplies.

Counseling May Be Lacking

Many people opposed to open adoption may feel this way because in their communities there is no source of help for open adoption mediation. With no third party intervention, the person with the most power is likely to be in control.

Until the final adoption papers are signed, the birthparents have that power. After the papers are signed, the adoptive parents are completely in charge. This is true in mediated adoptions, too, but through extensive counseling, adoption agencies and services can influence the use of that power.

Adoption case workers traditionally have had the power to decide which couples will become adoptive parents through their agencies. They have had the power to decide which baby each client will receive. Social workers who protest the most about the evils of open adoption may not want to give up the power they have held for so long because of closed adoption practices.

It is possible for couples to agree to open adoption in order to get a child. Once the final papers are signed, they may never contact the birthparents again. They want to forget she exists. This is not likely to happen if the adoptive parents have adequate counseling which provides insight into some of the needs and fears of birthparents. If they can develop real empathy for the birthparent, they are not likely to renege on their agreement.

A disadvantage with an independent adoption, even one done through an excellent adoption service, is that the adoptive parents in most states are not studied officially until *after* the child is placed. Some feel this is little better than no home study at all.

Mature Decisions Needed In Open Adoption

Offering a very young birthparent the opportunity to select an adoptive family for her baby and to be involved in deciding on a communication/visitation agreement means she will be asked to make adult decisions before she is an adult. She needs to decide on the kind of home she wants for her child, the kind of parenting techniques — a lot of big decisions, and it's tough.

Sister Maureen Joyce, Director of Community Maternity Services, Albany, New York, reports that her agency is carefully moving toward more and more openness in adoption. "I don't know how I feel about this," she said. "I know how teenagers feel when they are 15 and how they feel when they are 20 or 25 is radically different. I'm not sure all 15-year-olds can handle that total openness."

Sr. Maureen, who is open to change, continued, "We are at the point now when we don't really know what the effects will be. I'm certainly open to it, and I firmly believe we need to involve the birthparents as much as they can handle. I'm not trying to be the great protector, but neither am I trying to push them into something they simply are not ready to deal with."

Other social workers who advocate some form of open adoption are uneasy about the practice of birthparents meeting, perhaps choosing adoptive parents before the adoption is final. They feel this makes the adoptive couple feel as though they are on trial. For some people, they say, this would not be appropriate.

Some people are concerned about the effects on the child of open adoption. Won't she feel like she has two mothers? And won't this be damaging? Reuben Pannor, outspoken advocate of open adoption, claims this is ridiculous. He reminds us of the many positive relationships a child may have with a stepparent and/or other relatives and friends.

"The biggest hurdle to open adoption," Pannor asserts, "is getting the professionals in the field ready to accept the practice of open adoption and to work with it. Social workers and agencies don't want it because it would make their lives more complicated."

Adoptive Parents May Object

Adoptive parents who have had no experience with open adoption often are fearful of the process. Carolyn Fowler, Adoption and Foster Care Supervisor, Fairfax County Department of Social Services, Fairfax, Virginia, reports that her agency provides varying degrees of openness in adoption depending on the needs of the parties involved. "We talk to adoptive parents about the pain birthparents are experiencing. We teach them that no one owns a child, not even the child born to them," she explained.

"Adopted children come with a biological heritage which needs to be respected. We remind them the child really has two sets of parents, a concept that sometimes is shocking to them at first." Fowler recommends Silber and Speedlin's *Dear Birthmother* to her clients as a means of increasing empathy between adoptive and birthparents.

Linda West, Adoptions Coordinator, Children's Home Society of Mississippi, feels that most people are not healthy enough to handle all the dynamics of open adoption. She stresses the need, when considering open adoption, to assess both sets of parents' abilities to handle these dynamics. She thinks many birthparents have deepseated problems unrelated to the pregnancy, and that involving these young women in completely open adoptions is not wise.

West also worries that the child might be tremendously confused if there were too much contact between him and a second set of parents. She feels adoptive parents' fears of the birthparents snatching the child away would be even worse if they knew the birthmother had their name and address.

In one placement through their agency, the child's birthmother's parents were involved, and that didn't work well, according to West. The grandparents were not willing to let go of the child and would show up at his home at inopportune times. She said the adoptive parents finally had to move away.

Does Confidentiality Provide Protection?

The greatest foe of open adoption today undoubtedly is Bill Pierce, President, National Committee for Adoption. When asked about his opinion, he responded, "We don't like it (open adoption) at all. We think it's a very bad development. We think that down the line it will prove to be harmful for all those involved in the adoption circle."

Pierce is especially concerned about the possibility of fraud in adoption, fraud which he apparently believes is more likely to occur with openness. He spoke of attorneys using stand-in couples who meet the preferences of birthmothers, "young, cute, able to talk about their dogs and cats and horses," but who will not be the couple actually adopting the baby. He claims, also, that "fake girls" are meeting adoptive couples, young women who are gorgeously pregnant, but whose baby will not be the one to be adopted. (In truly open adoption where the birthparent(s) and the adoptive couple have ongoing contact, this practice would be impossible.)

"I believe one of the biggest reasons we need confidentiality is to protect people from the avarice and greed that exists in all of us," he warned. "There are some agencies where things are going on that I think verge on baby-selling, practices which are unethical. By and large we are able to avoid this because people don't meet. Otherwise it's bargaining-for-baby time and no holds barred." (One wonders how confidentiality can be considered a guarantee of trustworthiness.)

Pierce undoubtedly is correct in assuming that not everyone working in adoption is ethical. There is a risk of illegal financial gain for go-betweens and, occasionally, for the birthparent. Agencies generally offer more protection against such practices than do independent adoption practitioners.

This can happen. Honesty, however, is more likely to be a part of arrangements conducted in the open than in dealings veiled in secrecy.

Pierce is also concerned when open adoption is offered as an enticement to a young woman who otherwise would not consider an adoption plan. He feels she may not be ready for adoption if she cannot accept it within closed adoption planning.

Response to this concern depends on one's attitude toward birthparents. Are they intelligent, caring people who love their children enough to be concerned about the home into which they may be adopted? Or are they immature and uncaring individuals for whom someone else must make the decisions regarding their babies?

An Almost-Disrupted Adoption

Veronica's story appears to have a happy ending. She is satisfied that her baby is where she should be, and the adoptive parents have their long-awaited child. But it almost didn't happen. If Veronica had carried through with her plans to get her baby back, she and the baby would have, according to her comments, faced a difficult future.

Veronica would have had to survive on welfare, which she didn't want, or find a job paying enough to provide for daycare for Katrina as well as their other living expenses. She didn't feel she could do that.

Veronica placed her baby independently with no help from an adoption counselor. She told her doctor she thought adoption would be the best plan for her so he showed her a stack of resumes he kept in his desk drawer. She picked one, talked to the lawyer the doctor called, and met the couple.

Three weeks after Veronica had her baby, she tried unsuccessfully to get her back. Although she says now the adoption was right, she thinks both she and the adoptive parents could have had far less stress if counseling had been involved while she was pregnant, and if they could have communicated better with one another. It was a difficult situation for everyone involved.

Veronica's Story

Veronica shared her story about a year after her baby was born:

I was 16 when I got pregnant. Me and my boyfriend weren't talking much. I figured I didn't need his help — I'd do it on my own. I thought about abortion but I kept putting it off because I didn't believe I should do it. I decided it would be best to have the baby and give it up for adoption.

I found out about open adoption through my doctor. In his desk drawer he has letters and portfolios of couples who want to adopt. He put me in touch with this lawyer who handles adoptions.

We started interviewing couples in November when I was about four months pregnant. It would be me and my mom and dad and the lawyer. We would meet these couples at a coffeeshop and talk. The first four didn't seem right but I liked the fifth one. They already had a child, a four-year-old boy who was three months old when they adopted him.

After I talked with them I had this peaceful feeling that these were the people for my baby. Even though it wasn't my plan to get pregnant, I decided it was somehow planned to help these people.

After that we really didn't talk again except through the lawyer. There was a lot of confusion. Even the night Katrina was born, I didn't know if I wanted to give her up. A lot of times I called my best friend like I was going crazy. What shall I do...move out and keep this baby or what? She would never tell me what to do but she would remind me that I was awfully young, still in school, and that I had a lot of things to do before I tied myself down with a baby.

It's hard to get your mind and your emotions together. Your mind is telling you you should give this baby up while your emotions are telling you you can't do it. It's like rip and tear for nine months before and a year afterward. The week I had her I was a total wreck.

I think the worst emotional pull was the day after Katrina was born. I had actually seen her and held her.

Every time my parents and grandparents came to see me, I was asking them what I should do. I finally signed the medical release so she could leave the hospital with the adoptive parents.

Three weeks after she was born I called the lawyer back and said I wanted Katrina back — I wanted to bring her up myself. He tried to counsel me and tell me it was best for her to be with the adoptive parents. As young as I was, the lawyer didn't see why I would tie myself down with a baby. He obviously thought I was incapable of raising her. I didn't look at it that way — I carried her and I could raise her.

For two months we went through this. I learned later the lawyer never told the adoptive parents. Finally at three months the social worker called and asked if I wanted to set a court date. I told her I had been talking to the lawyer for two months and that I wanted Katrina back. The social worker said the people had never been informed, and that if I wanted to go through with it, I would have to go to court. I had waited too long to get her without court permission. That really threw me.

I called my mom at work. I was crying and I said, "I don't believe they did this to me. At three weeks I wanted Katrina back and nobody told these people. Now I have to go to court. They tell me I have to get a lawyer, find some way to pay him, draw up some papers." I called the legal aid people and they said, "We don't deal in family law." I couldn't get a lawyer because I had no way to pay him, and the lawyer I had totally ignored me. I felt deserted — he was taking sides with the adoptive parents.

The adoptive father actually called me at home and yelled at me. He said I was selfish and there was no way I was ever going to get Katrina back. He said his wife had no idea I wanted her back, that it would tear her apart. I said, "How do you think I felt when I left the hospital that day and left her there?" But he didn't see that. He just saw his side — that he wanted to keep her.

Value of Counseling

Then I started going to counseling. My mom works for a health clinic and I went to one of their counselors. I would go into these sessions and completely fall apart. At that point I was so wrapped up in wanting Katrina back that, to me, it was like everyone was against me, the lawyer, the adoptive parents, my family.

When I was in counseling I realized I wanted her back because it hurt me to leave her, not because of what it would do to her. Once I could figure that out, I could look at it in an objective way. That made it a lot easier to understand what I wanted to do.

I've seen a lot of girls younger than me have babies and keep them, and they don't have it any easier than I do. It might sound selfish and like I'm thinking of myself, but I think it took a lot of love and caring to give my baby up.

The real reason I decided to leave Katrina where she was is because I knew it could drag through the courts for a year. During that time the adoptive parents might have thought, "We'll feed her and we'll change her, but we don't want to get too attached to her because we might lose her." What would that do to Katrina? And what if they handed her to me a year later? Katrina wouldn't know who I was and that would be hard on her too. That's what made me decide to leave her where she was.

Two weeks before the court date, I called the social worker and said I would sign the final papers. I had gone out and gotten prices on apartments and furniture, and I decided I couldn't do this to my baby — live in the kinds of dumps I could afford.

On the day of the court hearing, it was pouring rain and we had parked two blocks away. I was soaking wet when I went in. I stood up in court, and I had no lawyer.

The adoptive father walked over to me and said, "I apologize for what I said to you on the phone. I'm not here to fight you." And I said, "I'm not here to fight you. I'm going to sign." And then he started to cry.

The social worker hadn't told them I would sign and they thought I was there to fight them for the baby. Better communication could have cut out some of the pain.

It seemed to me like everybody pampered the adoptive parents like they were the ones going through the trauma, they were the ones who were confused. It was like I had given up the baby, now I was out of the picture. At least my parents were supportive. They were willing to talk with me about my feelings.

The day I came home from court I was at a loss. I didn't know how I felt. On the one hand I was happy because Katrina was with them. I knew they were happy with her and she was getting good care. But on the other hand I felt such a loss, like somebody had died. But I feel all right now.

Because Veronica agreed to counseling, she began to realize some of the problems she might face if she kept her baby. She finally made her decision, a decision she can live with and which seems to be best for Katrina and the adoptive parents.

People opposed to open adoption may use this story as an example of an almost-disrupted adoption. Because she knew where her child was placed, Veronica came close to demanding her back. If the adoption had been a closed agency adoption, she would not have had this opportunity.

However, if Veronica had placed through a good agency, she would have undergone counseling during her pregnancy. She might have chosen to keep her baby. She might, if she were offered both options, have chosen an adoption plan which was open, or one which was completely confidential. Who knows?

Chances are good, however, that with adequate counseling, she would have been able to make a firm decision without creating so much stress for herself and her baby's adoptive parents.

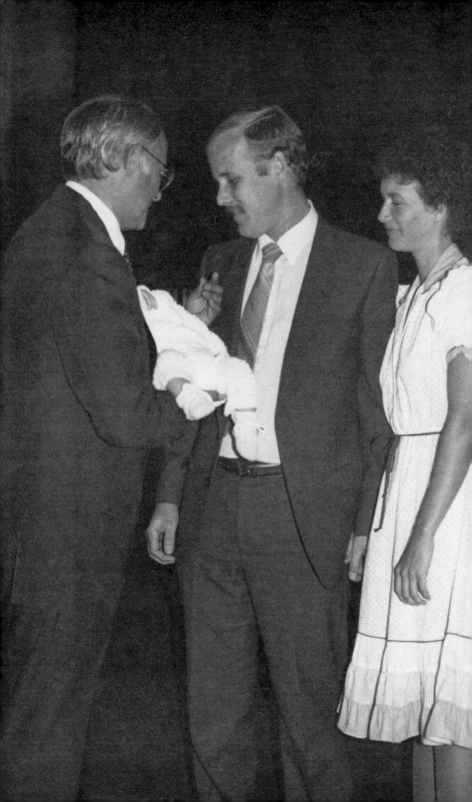

10

Open Adoption and Family Services — The Mediation Approach

Mediation is the byword at Open Adoption and Family Services, Inc., a licensed adoption agency in Eugene, Oregon. Serving only Oregon families, the agency is like many others in insisting on extensive counseling for adoptive parents and birthparents. But the counseling goes one step further, according to Director and founder Jeanne Etter.

Mediation means both sets of parents negotiate their open adoption agreement with the help of a professionally trained mediator. Each then signs a formal document outlining their agreement, and this is attached to the adoption decree.

"Mediation not only serves everyone's interests more completely and fairly, but it also makes certain that the agreement will stand the test of time," Etter explained.

Founder Is Adoptive Parent

Like many others working with adoptions, Etter and her husband are adoptive parents. Their daughter was ten months old when she came into their home. Her birthmother found the Etters through a friend of a friend. The birthmother felt she couldn't raise her baby daughter, but she wasn't going to release her to an agency and lose contact with her.

For a month the Etters and the child's birthmother talked. All three felt continued contact would be best for the baby, but what were the guidelines to be for that contact?

"We worked it out, but looking back, we think a third party with an objective point of view would have helped. To have had a mediator would have made a big difference," Etter commented.

A couple of years later, a pregnant friend asked Etter to help her plan her child's adoption. "As a friend, I helped her, but some things didn't work out as she wanted," Etter admitted. "Then I decided you don't do a little bit of adoption work. You either do it professionally and cover all the bases or not at all. It's the birthparents who suffer when someone is not doing it professionally."

The next time someone came to Etter for help, she decided to make a career switch. She had been an educator of parents and young children, and was trained in divorce mediation. She soon realized the mediation process used in divorce cases was also relevant to adoption.

The critical thing about adoption as compared to divorce mediation is that in adoption, the agreement between the parties is totally voluntary. Each has a choice, and each can pull out at any time until the final decision is made and the legal papers are signed. In divorce mediation, this is not the case.

State Licensed Agency

Open Adoption and Family Services became a state licensed adoption agency in 1985. By mid-1986 Etter had supervised almost 60 adoptions, and the agency's case load was increasing. "At one point we had more birthparents then would-be adoptive parents," she reported. She believes this is because more people with unplanned pregnancies are choosing open adoption who otherwise would opt for abortion if closed adoption were the only other alternative to parenthood.

Many people, both birthparents and adoptive parents, are interested in some form of open adoption. However, some want contact with confidentiality at first. They may choose not to exchange full names and addresses, and to use the agency as the go-between.

Clients who begin with confidentiality often move on to fully open adoption later, according to Etter. "If they are not sure how open they want to be, it's a good idea to start slowly," she said. "You can always move to more openness but you can't go back."

Birthmothers who come to the agency for help are encouraged to examine their options thoroughly. Each receives a sheet of questions which asks first that she consider her own wishes concerning this child. Does she like the idea of being a full-time parent and does she really want to take this responsibility? Does parenthood fit in well with her personal and future plans?

She is also asked to consider the desires of her parents and of her baby's father. What emotional and other support does she have?

If she decides to raise her child, she considers the realities of parenting as she talks with her counselor/mediator. If parenting is her decision, the counselor/mediator helps her contact community resources she may need in order to develop parenting skills and plan her life with her baby. At least three-fourths of the agency's pregnant clients make the decision to parent their babies.

Consideration of Open Adoption

If she chooses to consider open adoption, she is asked to respond to the following questions:

Are you ready to let go of a parenting relationship with your child?

Is adoption a decision that is right for you or do you think adoption is what you ought to do?

Would you be comfortable with an on-going relationship with the adoptive family and the child?

Being poor is often temporary, adoption is forever. Are you comparing yourself unfavorably with what an adoptive family can offer?

Are you giving yourself credit for your ability to be a good parent?

If adoption is your choice, are you prepared for the sense of loss the separation will bring?

Do you have supportive caring people who will go through the adoption with you?

Do you have plans for afterward when you are no longer responsible for the child?

If open adoption is still her decision, she learns of the choices she has within adoption. Is she ready to let go of a parenting relationship with the child? At the same time, would she be comfortable with an on-going relationship with the adoptive family and the child?

The counselor/mediator also helps her plan her life after her child is placed with the adoptive family. She needs to have supportive, caring people with her at this time, and she needs to have plans for her own life.

Choosing A Family

With help from her counselor/mediator, she decides on the kind of adoptive family she wants her child to have. They talk about values, preferred lifestyles, interests, religion, child care plans, and other relevant topics.

She then studies the various adoptive families registered with the agency. At this time, she sees only non-identifying information about each couple. When she chooses a couple, her counselor/mediator sets up a meeting.

She, the couple, and the counselor/mediator meet. If they decide to work out an adoption plan together, they begin discussing their options. How open do they want to be? Do they want to communicate directly or through an intermediary? What kind and frequency of visitation rights

will the birthparents have? How often and in what way
will the adoptive parents communicate with her?

As they work out their agreement with help from the
counselor/mediator, they talk about financial responsibility.
What expenses must the adoptive parents pay? Usually
this will include medical expenses not covered by
insurance, agency counseling and mediation costs, and
possibly some living expenses during pregnancy.

If the birthmother decides to keep her child, the contract
states that she is liable for all of these costs. She must pay
back to the adoptive parents any of her expenses they
have already paid. Under Oregon law, it is permissable to
require reimbursement of such expenses if the adoption
does not occur, according to Etter.

Mediation Agreement Developed

The mediation is patterned on a general open adoption
agreement prepared by Open Adoption and Family
Services. This is available in two forms, one for adoption
with no exchange of surnames or addresses, and the
other, for completely open adoption.

The agreement covers visitation, communication, and
financial responsibilities, but it may be altered as the
adoptive parents and birthparent(s) see fit. When the
agreement is completed to the satisfaction of all parties, it
is attached to the Petition to Adopt, and becomes part of
the court record.

"We do not know how this agreement would stand up
in court if it were challenged by either side," Etter
acknowledged. "We have never had anybody on either
side break their agreement, and I think the reason is that
it is a very easy agreement to keep.

"The birthparents have the option of visiting but not the
requirement. It's always at the convenience of the adoptive
parents. It's different from a divorce agreement where the
visit may be every other week. The visits are always with
the adoptive family as a group, not with the child
separately. They can even agree to have the

counselor/mediator with them during these visits. There is
no pressure on anyone to do anything uncomfortable.

"While the agreement is easy to follow, challenging it in
court would be hard," Etter asserts. "If the birthparents
break it, they lose everything. If the adoptive parents
break it, they could end up in court with a judge
deciding, and they don't want that."

Counseling For Adoptive Couples

To become an adoptive parent applicant at Open
Adoption and Family Services, couples attend an intake
meeting. They have a home study which involves
counseling. There is additional counseling along the way,
and they are encouraged to attend adoptive parent
support meetings. They also receive post-adoption
counseling.

The home study involves a visit to the home. They
submit their autobiographies, family health history,
financial statements, and other materials. They specify the
kinds of children they will accept — infants only, older
children, special needs children, minorities. They also
describe what they have to offer to a child.

Agency costs to the adoptive parents total about $2,100
which includes court reports, home study, mediation,
intake, and post-adoption counseling for the birthparents.
Adoptive parents also pay legal fees and perhaps medical
costs and some living expenses for the birthmother. This
usually totals between $3,000 and $7,000.

The agency depends on donations and foundation
grants to provide free counseling to pregnant women in
need.

The agency's Fact Sheet includes the following
reassurances for those who are nervous about open
adoption: "The adoptive parents become the sole legal
parents at the time the child is placed in their home and
the adoption is permanent at that time. Open adoption
simply means that the birthparents will have the peace of

mind that comes from knowing how the child is doing over the years."

"Everyone needs to know that adoption and what it means to our society is changing," concludes Etter. "Instead of adoption rates going down, down, down, I feel sure adoption will be chosen more often if openness is one of the alternatives available. Adoptive parents need to know that mediated open adoption need not be threatening. This is an alternative, and it's happening more and more widely.

"Birthparents need to know this is an alternative, and people in other areas must make this option available."

The agency has designed a three-year model project and research program to study the effects of mediation on adoption. The study is scheduled for completion in 1989. Etter also offers training in mediated open adoption to professionals interested in setting up similar programs in other areas.

Wanda Sue's Story

Wanda Sue was not a teenage mother. She was married at 19 and had her first baby when she was 20. The marriage didn't work out, and at 22, she was a divorced, single mother.

Her second pregnancy was especially heart-breaking. She was raped one evening on her way home from work at a neighborhood restaurant. Several weeks later she found to her horror that she was pregnant. She shared her story:

I don't believe in abortion so I had two choices, adoption or keeping. I knew there were a lot of things I couldn't give the baby. My son gets to spend time with his father, but this baby wouldn't have that. I also wondered if, on an unconscious level, I might start resenting the baby because of the rape. I'm still having problems dealing with that.

My perception of adoption was horrible, like the Dark Ages. You have the baby, they take it away, and you never see it, never know who it's with. That was my idea of adoption.

My doctor suggested I call Open Adoption and Family Services. When the counselor explained open adoption to me, I knew right away that was what I wanted. I would be in control, I could choose the family. For one thing, I knew it had to be a Christian home. That was important to me.

I went home and prayed a lot — should I decide on adoption? When I woke up one morning, I was full of peace and knew adoption was the right answer.

I was already seven months pregnant when I went in. It's better to go in sooner, but we had plenty of time. I read through a bunch of letters describing adoptive parents and I picked two or three out. Then they showed me their autobiographies and I picked Sally and Stewart. It took a lot of reading and considering, but when I saw their materials, I knew that was the family for my baby.

About a week after I made my decision, I met Sally and Stewart at the agency office. That first meeting was long and a little hard. I felt nervous and anxious and I know they did too. Once we started talking, it wasn't too bad.

I could tell right away they were the couple I wanted. I saw them two or three other times, but basically communicated through the agency until I had the baby.

When Trent was born, I wanted to spend some time with him by myself. I called the agency and asked them to have Sally and Stewart wait a couple of hours before coming in. I spent a lot of time with Trent the two days I was there and I'm glad I did. I needed to say hello before I had to say goodbye.

Sally and Stewart came in and spent time with me and Trent. That was hard, but it was also neat to sit there and watch these people, knowing I had made their dreams come true.

When I went home, it was hard. It's a real loss, but a different kind of loss. I know Trent is still out there but I can't see him. I talk to the counselor every once in a while, and I got a letter and pictures recently from Sally. He's two months old now.

I have visitation rights, but we didn't exchange last names. The visits will be in the Open Adoption office. Some do exchange names and addresses, but in my heart I realized if I knew where he was, I'd be over there. Our agreement can always be changed if we all want to do it, and I know they're open to me visiting later if I want to.

It was a good experience for me. It hurt and it was hard. I'd much rather have kept Trent and raised him myself, but I knew it wouldn't be best for him or for me.

This has been such a blessing, to give something to a family who has prayed for him for years. I've answered somebody's prayers, and that's a nice feeling.

Sally and Stewart Become Parents

Sally is tall and slim. She loves to sew and makes all her clothes. Before she and Stewart adopted six-year-old Annalee, Sally taught in a pre-school. Stewart teaches math in their local high school and coaches Little League baseball.

They adopted Annalee when they lived in Wisconsin. Her adoption was closed with no exchange of information between them and the adoptive parents. Over the years, they have sent letters and pictures to the birthmother through the agency but have had no contact whatsoever with her. As Sally puts it, she's not a reality to them. Trent's adoption is very different:

Sally: We heard good things about Open Adoption and Family Services and we checked them out with the Better Business Bureau. So I called and made an appointment. Stewart, Annalee and I went in together and we visited with the counselor. Then we wrote our autobiographies and filled out the other papers.

We expected a long wait, but Wanda Sue chose us right after we submitted our application. We went to Eugene to meet her, and she told us what she expected of us as parents. Then we went outside and took a walk while she talked with the social worker.

We went back and Judy (counselor/mediator) asked if we liked Wanda Sue. We thought she was really nice. In fact, it was a wonderful experience. We all decided to go ahead with the adoption plan.

Stewart: We saw Wanda Sue at the agency two more times. It was her choice to remain anonymous. We worked out a few things together, like the expenses. We paid the agency fee, Trent's birth expenses, and part of Wanda Sue's counseling before and after she had the baby.

To work out our agreement, we all sat down together with Judy and went over the basic form. Wanda Sue spoke up and said what she wanted and we said what we wanted. What we didn't like we adjusted and made a second one. Wanda Sue did the same with her changes.

It was amazing the way everything worked out, just like a puzzle.

Sally: One day Wanda Sue called through the agency and invited us to meet her at the doctor's office so we could hear the baby's heartbeat. We took Annalee again, drove to Eugene, and met Wanda Sue's three-year-old son.

Our counselor/mediator called us a couple of hours after Trent was born. We drove over and went in. The baby was lying next to Wanda Sue, and her mother was sitting beside her. She said, "Would you like to hold your son?" I said "Yes," and it was a beautiful moment.

Then I called Wanda Sue the next day and asked if she would rather be with the baby alone that day and she said "Yes," so we didn't go down. I think that was special for her. It gave her time to be with him.

Stewart: When we went down the first time I thought, "I'd sure like to bring him home right now." Then I got home and the Lord said, "Don't be selfish. You'll have this boy all your life." We think it's something special, the best gift we could ever receive.

You know, I was a little scared when we first went to the hospital to see Trent, but both Wanda Sue and her mother were very loving and understanding. Sometimes I put myself in Wanda Sue's place and it makes a difference. You realize what a sacrifice she's making. If she didn't know where Trent is or who his parents are, it could leave a real scar on her life.

Sally: I'm glad we can share with Trent the joy we felt that day because it was a neat experience, so wonderful, having Wanda Sue give us this child. It's something we can share with Trent and help him realize his birthmother and birthgrandparents did this together.

Stewart: It gives us peace of mind because we did it with their blessing. That's important.

11

Two Adoption Stories — One Birthmother

Erin was working in an independent adoption service when I met her. She is a political activist who cares a great deal about people and about social issues. In her late twenties now, she has placed two children for adoption, one six years ago when she was 22, and one six months before we talked.

Her son's placement was through an agency and was supposed to be totally closed. She had a completely different experience with her daughter's adoption. She and the baby's birthfather were deeply involved in planning it and total openness was important to both of them.

Both stories offer valuable insight into the adoption drama. So do the experiences shared by Janice and Jim who adopted Erin and Bernardo's daughter. Bernardo also shares his version of the story.

Closed Adoption Six Years Ago

It's very significant, I think, that I'm able to speak from the birthmother point of view on both open and closed adoption. I think I see more closely the advantages in open adoption than does someone who has never seen the other side.

When my son was born six years ago, I knew I wanted adoption. If the baby's father had pushed abortion, I would have considered it. I was 22 and had no support whatsoever. I was not the least bit prepared to be a mother. I had no friends who were parents. I knew my family wouldn't accept adoption — all these reasons pointed to abortion, I suppose. But his father was a middle-aged macho European who was delighted that he could still make babies.

I said, "You know we would never make it as a couple. You're comfortable in your marriage and you don't need a scandal. Neither of us is ready to parent this baby." So we decided on adoption, and mostly he was supportive. Toward the end he said, "You can't prove I'm the father. What if I say I'm not, and won't sign the papers?" I said, "You know me. I would take it to court and you don't want that scandal." But we talked it out and he signed the papers.

The first thing I did after we decided on adoption was look in the phone book for someone to call. I thought I made a choice because I chose one of several agencies. I knew nothing about open adoption then. The social worker let me look at descriptions of families, descriptions written by social workers with no identifying information whatsoever. "He is blond and 6'3", and she is brunette and likes the outdoors."

But somehow I knew the connection had to be deeper that what I saw on that paper. The birthfather and I finally selected a family, but some part of me knew I wouldn't let my baby go unless I knew where he was going.

And it happened. Before he was born, the agency made what they felt was an error, and I knew everything about the adoptive family — their name, address, telephone number, and where he worked. I had all this information and I knew about the biological daughter they had. This is where I started getting out of the physical reality and into miracles because that's the only way I survived emotionally. All the support I had was nothing compared to knowing where my baby was.

Throughout these years I have fantasized about calling up and saying, "I'm a new babysitter in the neighborhood" or "I'm doing a survey for Beechnut baby food" or simply cruising by his house. I didn't, but just knowing I could helped so much.

When he was born I had to fight even to see him in the hospital. My social worker helped me or I wouldn't have seen him at all. When he was a month old I finally got the hospital picture. That was the only thing I had, and he looked exactly like his father when he was born. So for six years I had fantasies about this little dark-skinned, dark-eyed kid.

Then after I had Heather and it was such a wonderful experience, I called the social worker I had had six years before. I told her about Heather, and said I'd like to have a current picture of my son. She had been an advocate for me when he was born, but she told me now she couldn't possibly get me a picture.

Contact With First Adoptive Father

So I decided I had to contact his adoptive family. I tried to decide whether to write them, call the mother at home because I knew she didn't work, or call the dad at work. First I decided to try to find his dad at work. I prepared myself for this long incredible search because people change jobs all the time.

I called his office and they put me through to him within five minutes. I said, "This is Erin Kathleen and I'm your son's birthmother." He said, "Wow, I knew I recognized that name. I have people in the office, but I'll call you right back." And he did. We talked for two hours, and one of my fears was justified. Our political views were extremely different, but once we got that out of the way, we respected each other.

I learned that he had used the same agency error to learn who I was. He had wanted to contact me but his wife and friends told him not to for all the usual reasons. He told his wife I had called but she didn't want to meet me.

We had lunch together a few days later and talked and talked. When he handed me a picture of my son, the first I had seen since his birth picture, he said, "Are you ready for this?" And it was a real ceremony. He gave me the picture and the world stopped turning. I was looking at my own face! I can't explain to you what that did in my heart. He has his dad's olive skin but my eyes, my face, my cheekbones. Then he showed me all kinds of other pictures, too, and it was just lovely.

I talked with him about open adoption and took him some materials. He shared them with his wife, but at this point she doesn't want to meet me. I dream that she will call me. I think she will.

Second Time — Completely Different

Erin's second pregnancy and adoption plan were completely different:

This time when I realized I was pregnant I knew what I wanted. Although I lived about 300 miles away, I contacted Jeanne Etter because I knew she could help me with my open adoption plan. She sent me some letters. I went through them all, but wasn't sure I found what I was looking for. She called me and I poured my heart out to her, how I wanted parents who were political activists as I was, that I wanted my child in this kind of atmosphere.

She said, "This is your baby, this is your choice, and you should lay out all the requirements you have in your heart for the parents of this child." Then she said, "Have you looked at Jim and Janice's letter? They seem to be everything you're looking for." I went back to it, and Jeanne sent me more information about them, and I was quite sure.

Adoption Agreement Developed

Bernardo (the birthfather) and I worked with a counselor/mediator near my home while Jim and Janice spent several hours with one from the agency in their town.

We talked by phone several times and I visited Jim and Janice two weekends during my pregnancy. We talked a lot and we put our adoption agreement in writing. I think this solidifies the love, the respect, and the trust that the parties involved have for each other. My relationship with Jim and Janice has gotten to be that of friends anyway, so I don't think there will ever come a time when we'll have to go back to our written agreement and say, "But you said this."

Our contract says I have four visits during her first year, two the next, and one each year from then on. We agreed to send current pictures, and that we would notify each other when we move or anything serious happens to any of us. Should they die and a guardian take over for Heather, that guardian would also be bound by all of these agreements.

Heather's birth was very special. Jim and Janice were with me and so was my mother. Bernardo was there part of the time, and his mother came to the hospital later that day.

We co-parented for the first few days. We lived together, I breastfed her, and we took turns getting up at night. On the fifth day we had a ceremony with all the closest people involved with all of us. We sat around and everybody talked. Then we passed Heather around and everybody held her. It was lovely.

When Jim and Janice left with Heather the next day, I said they didn't need to call or write to me until October when Heather would be three months old and I would visit them. I said I wanted this to be the time for them to become a family. I think because I had given them that option, they didn't need it. When they called when Heather was a month old, it was such a joy.

As we had agreed, I visited for a weekend when Heather was three months old. That was the right amount of time. I didn't sleep at their house, but I was there most of the time.

I feel I can pick up the phone and call Jim and Janice any time. Part of that is it rests on my shoulders to know when enough is enough. We talk with each other two or three times a month now. For the first four monthly birthdays they called me which was a total surprise.

My daughter lives in Eugene, Oregon, with her family. She is six months old now, and it means so much to be able to call and ask how she is, to know that she is well, she's safe, she's happy, she is where she should be. Jim and Janice have the patience, the stability, and material resources, they have the desire to parent that I don't have.

I always wanted her, I always had the desire to carry her and to give birth to her. I also wanted her to be able to grow up in the optimal environment. Staying with me, she wouldn't have had that.

Sometimes people say to me, "Do you ever want to have your own children?" I say, "I have two of my own children." People have attitudes that of course they're entitled to have, but so many of them are based on myth. I feel I almost have a duty to correct these, to be very carefully tuned in to every person who talks about adoption so I can help them see reality.

Like "to give up" — you don't give up your child, you don't have to build a wall. That's the choice of open adoption, there's no pretense about it. But people get scared. Like my son's adoptive father said, "I know we're on a honeymoon right now. It's an amazing relationship, but eventually I expect there will be some problems." I said of course there will. We're human, and any relationship between humans is going to include problems. But when you have a chance to build a relationship of love and trust from the very beginning, from the very first possible moment, problems that come up can be worked out.

Bernardo's Experiences

Bernardo is Hispanic and had spent two years in Central America before his baby's birth. He is a ruggedly handsome, bearded, thoughtful-looking man. He cooperated with the adoption plan, but it was an extremely difficult decision for him:

I had mixed feelings about this whole thing. I felt angry, I almost felt set-up. We had a short affair, and when I realized Erin was pregnant, I felt cold and strange inside.

I knew we would not stay together because we're not very compatible. She went back to California and we kept in touch through letters. We lived about 400 miles apart. I worked hard at not getting angry because it was too late for that.

I had a choice of claiming the infant and taking it before adoption, but I couldn't raise the baby myself. My mother wanted her but I remembered my life when I was growing up. I didn't want that for my child. I had been away from California for two years and didn't know anyone who would raise the baby here. Keeping the baby was not feasible.

Erin made the adoption plan but she kept telling me I could participate. I read about Jim and Janice's background and I thought they were a good choice. We worked out a contract, and they first tried to restrict my visits. I'd say, "Don't worry about that. Let's try to establish a relationship, let's be friends." It worked. Jim and Janice contact me more than I contact them.

That ceremonial thing after Heather was born — I felt like running out with the kid and not going through with it. I know it was good for Jim and Janice, the symbolism of it, but it was all planned by Erin. I felt lots of anguish, like a knot in my gut.

But the adoption was the best thing. I'm glad it's Jim and Janice, knowing how much they love the baby. I still block out feelings, but consciously I know it was the best thing.

Most of my friends are very negative about the adoption. Most of them think it was a horrible thing to do and I live with that. But I have my own ways of dealing with that.

I think the open adoption is a good idea, but it's hard on both parties. If it had been anonymous, I would always feel the guilt. That hidden guilt would be worse than having it out in the open. I do feel guilty for what I did, for not having been the man and doing the ideal, taking care of my child like in the movies.

At least it's not a secret which will work against me. At least it's always out in the open and I have to deal with it. If I had to choose again, I'd choose open adoption because a secret is the worst part.

I know this was the best thing. I'm glad it's Jim and Janice. They are very beautiful people, but the pain is still there.

Jim And Janice's Script

About the time Erin relinquished her first baby for adoption, Jim and Janice decided to start their family. But the first year passed, and the second, and they didn't conceive. They share their story:

Janice: Because of our infertility, we went through all kinds of medical stuff for four years. That got tiring and traumatic. Then we went to a Resolve conference. At that meeting I got upset at a presentation put on by an agency. They made it sound as though after our four years of total powerlessness, this agency would continue having all the power if we did decide to adopt.

I didn't want to continue that powerlessness with adoption. I felt strongly I didn't want to go to a traditional agency. I just couldn't take it.

Jim: We went to several pre-adopt classes and considered adopting foreign or hard-to-place children. Then we heard about Jeanne Etter's agency and we connected with them fairly quickly.

Janice: There was a lot of counseling there for the birthmothers before they chose a family. They were likely to be pretty committed by the time they got to the choosing point. They also got counseling after the placement.

Jim: We first heard about Erin almost three months before she delivered.

Janice: The first phone call was interesting. The counselor/mediator had set the exact time we were to call. When Erin picked up the phone, she said, "Hi Mom, Hi, Dad."

Erin came up here and we met her in a counseling session. She had already had two or three hours of counseling when we arrived. At that time we all decided we would go through with it. Then Erin spent two days with us, two very intense days. We wrote our adoption agreement and focused on how we wanted the adoption to go. We had started it in that first counseling session.

Jim: That was an important time because we had to deal with our feelings about how open our adoption was going to be. We were working with someone we had gotten to know pretty quickly but hadn't known long. Those two days really tested our willingness to be honest and to talk about how we were feeling about the kind of relationship we wanted and could handle.

We talked about two general areas — the birth and the visits afterward. We settled on four visits the first year, two the next, and one each year after that. We all agreed to this schedule.

During this time we also worked out a visitation schedule with Heather's birthfather. Bernardo agreed with Erin that adoption was the best plan, but he wanted to be involved, too. He and Erin worked with the same counselor/mediator.

Janice: I preferred that they not visit during the first three months. I wanted us to be sole parents with no ambiguity. I didn't want contact. As it turned out, we called Erin on Heather's first three monthly birthdays and I think she was pleased.

Intense Contact After Birth

Jim: Erin wanted to nurse and to have a relationship with her baby at the beginning. It took us awhile to feel comfortable with that. We worked out the limits we felt there had to be. We ended up understanding that what Erin felt at the time was important to all of us.

It was scary because there were unknowns involved. But we had a lot of confidence that Erin would not change her mind. We believed her when she said this was something she wanted to give her baby and it was part of the process of letting go.

Janice: I don't think we ever worried that Erin would change her mind. Our friends and families were on pins and needles. We knew those first days would be very intense. We worked out the number of days we would be together and when we would start feeding Heather formula.

Being with Erin while she delivered meant a lot to us. Then we were all together at my sister's house for three days. Erin went back to her place for another two days but visited us a lot. It was a clear change, a transition period for her to get used to us being with Heather.

Presentation Ceremony

Janice: The ceremony was a suggestion from the counselor/mediator, and that suggestion alone paid for her time. We were all sort of dreading the point when we would part and go back to Eugene — groaning and moaning about how we were going to deal with that. The counselor/mediator said, "Well, why don't you make it some kind of a celebration, something that you can plan and look forward to?" We all jumped at that.

There were about 15 people in my sister's house — Erin's friends, our friends. It was an incredible experience. Each person held Heather while she or he talked about what this situation meant to them. It ended with Jim and me, and then Erin and Bernardo talking about how we each felt. It was really heavy duty, amazing stuff.

Bernardo was the last one to talk. Then he and Erin together brought Heather over to us. He said, "Aqui le entregamos noestra hija." (We bring you our daughter.) Erin said, as they handed Heather to us, "We give you your daughter."

Jim: It brought out the best of all the people there. I felt much the same way at our wedding.

Janice: What makes all this so remarkable is what a wonderful child she is, such a joy every day. She's delightful.

People can't understand how I could have handled the stuff at my sister's house with the nursing, the visits. I wouldn't have understood it either before I went through it. Now I wouldn't have missed it.

I think the counseling helped a lot. I also think our situation is somewhat unique. Erin is a little older than most birthmothers and she has had a lot of life experiences which have put her where she is.

Jim: I know the counseling was important. We weren't totally on our own in working things out. Even though we were able to work out a lot for ourselves, the counseling gave a context in which to do it.

It was important to us to be honest about what we were feeling as we were negotiating our agreement. All of us said things that were hard to say, things we were afraid of. We didn't always get what we wanted — it was give and take. But it is important to get to the point where we could be honest about what we were feeling. This has continued — it's hard and it takes work, but I think it has paid off. I don't think any of us like lots of unspoken issues running around.

Janice: That's where mediation can help. There's a third party there helping us all understand the other person has feelings. If you are desperate, you'll say anything. The birthmother will be in the same position. She wants you to like her and she may be willing to say anything. But the stakes are too high. What makes open adoption work is the birthmother knows where her child is and that she's OK.

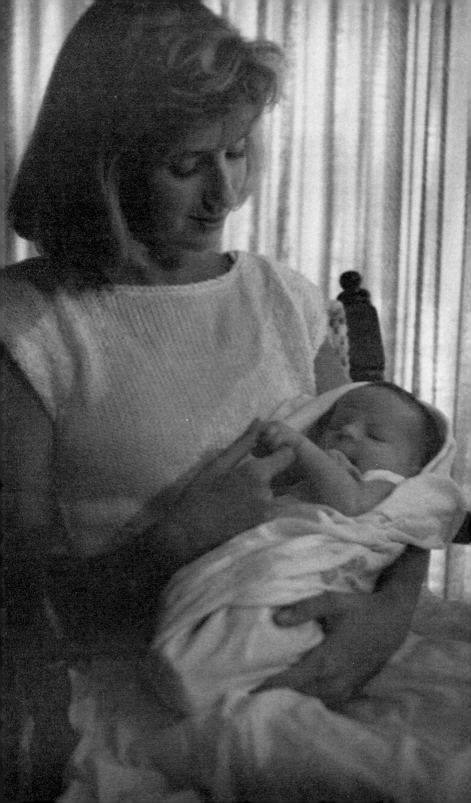

12

New Beginning —
A Better Way

Sue Monarch is a birthmother who released her son for adoption 22 years ago. She has experienced the grief, the pain that came from not knowing where her child was, whether he was alive or dead, or anything about his adoptive family. Finally, three years ago she started searching for him and found him.

"I discovered a lot of other people searching," she said, "experiencing bitterness at the system, and I even felt bitterness at first between my son's family and mine. They felt threatened, afraid I would take him away. We were all thinking of him as an infant rather than what he really was, an 18-year-old! When we all started looking at this realistically, we became friends.

"This was why I started New Beginning. I was sure there must be a better way to do adoptions," she explained.

Adoption Service Since 1983

Monarch and Jackie Radus started the non-profit adoption service in 1983. During the first three years they facilitated the adoption of 77 babies. They usually have 35-40 couples in their files at one time, but turnover is fairly rapid.

New Beginning, Santa Ana, California, is an adoption
service (not a licensed agency) for pregnant girls
considering adoption. "We give them all the options,"
Monarch explained. "If we feel she wants to keep her
child, we will refer her to the various resources she needs.
If she is interested in adoption — and most are by the time
they get to us — she looks at our resources and chooses
one or more families."

The birthparent can interview as many families as she
wishes, one at a time, then choose the one she wants to
rear her child. She and the family together will determine
the degree of openness they want, whether they will
exchange pictures, meet, maintain an on-going relationship
— or have no contact at all.

"Perhaps two percent choose closed adoption," Monarch
explained. "Last night a young girl came in, looked at the
resumes, and said she doesn't want to meet the adoptive
couple. We always leave the door open so that she may
have contact at a later date if she wishes. Some girls who
don't want to meet the adoptive parents regret it four or
five years down the line and wish they had.

"From a legal standpoint, having this opportunity
depends on trust because there is no legal form now
which will guarantee anything like this. So far, everyone
we've worked with has honored what they promised to
do. I think this is because it's open and nobody feels
threatened. They feel comfortable with the girl and her
position."

Birthmothers at New Beginning are expected to attend
ten counseling sessions, some before and some after
delivery. The adoptive couple pays for this service
because, as Monarch points out, it is in their best interest
to do so. The birthmother is going through the normal
grieving process for the loss of the baby and she needs
help in understanding that this doesn't mean she made
the wrong decision.

When adoptive couples prepare their resumes, Monarch
and Radus strongly encourage the use of lots of pictures.

They say most of the birthmothers skim the written
material but carefully examine the pictures.

Birthparent and Couple May Become Friends

"When she meets the couple, she learns more about
them," Monarch commented. "It also gives the couple a
chance to meet the birthmother and they, too, gain needed
information. How sure is she with her adoption plan? By
meeting and talking with her, a lot of their concerns are
talked through.

"In fact, a lot of our couples and the birthmothers who
choose them become good friends and do a lot of things
together. We have never had a girl live with the couple
and we don't really encourage this. If she stays with them,
does she continue after delivery or does she lose both the
family and the baby?

Birthparents, of course, are never charged anything for
the services they receive from New Beginning. Adoptive
parents pay a fee ($800 in 1986) when they sign up for the
service and an additional amount ($2000) when the
birthparent chooses them. If for any reason the adoption
does not go through, the latter fee is refunded. In
addition to the New Beginning fees, the adoptive couple
pays the legal expenses of the adoption plus pregnancy-
related expenses incurred by the birthmother. This
includes any medical expenses not covered by insurance.

"Once in a while people say we charge too much for
what we do," Monarch admitted. "But we usually see the
girl when she is three months pregnant, take her to all
her doctor's appointments, and take her to counseling.
Sometimes we pick her up at 2 A.M. and take her to the
hospital and coach her through labor and delivery.

"One girl came to see us who wanted money, a lot of
money. She was going to have a baby in about four
months and she wanted adoptive parents who would pay
her $1000 per month rent, buy her a car, a new wardrobe,
and $2300 worth of furniture. We told her we couldn't
help her.

"Girls who decide they want open adoption feel really wonderful about the people they have chosen and they don't want to do anything to hurt them. And the adoptive couple are so careful not to hurt her. The birthmother sometimes writes to me and says, 'I don't want to make them nervous and think I want the baby back, but I would like to give her this gift. I take the message to the adoptive couple, and they usually wind up telling each other it's OK and getting in direct contact."

Counseling for Adoptive Parents

"We send all the adoptive parents to an adoption information seminar and we pay for it. We also practically browbeat them when they come to us to convince them of the risks involved. Even in the best circumstances it is possible that the birthmother will change her mind. They all know this is a possibility," Monarch explained.

In addition to the 77 birthmothers who have placed their babies for adoption through New Beginning, about 13 first made an adoption plan, then changed their minds, seven before delivery and six afterward. Most of these decided against adoption within the first week after delivery, but one changed her mind six weeks after the baby was placed with the adoptive couple.

Sometimes, according to Monarch, a couple will go to counseling after "their" birthmother changes her mind and they "lose" a baby. Occasionally they ask that their resume not be shown again until they are ready to trust again. "We had one couple who became very close to the birthmother. They took her on vacation, had her stay at their home for a few days at a time. They were with her during delivery.

"Then she changed her mind the next day. But they felt it coming during the last week before birth. She changed her mind, I think, because throughout her pregnancy she had no parental support, but in the end she got it all. At the last minute her parents flew in here and urged her to go back home with the baby. They promised to help her.

"The adoptive couple told me they were ready to try again for another baby, but they might not want to be quite so open this time. But they're like that. They'll want to be close again."

Three Siblings, Two Families

Not all the children whose adoptions are facilitated by New Beginning are infants. Monarch described a young woman with three children aged 3 months, two years, and three years. She decided to give up all three for adoption.

Monarch showed her resumes and she interviewed at least 20 families. She wanted the little one to go to one family and the other two to another family. She felt the older two, a boy and a girl, would be treated equally and loved equally. However, she was concerned that if the baby were placed with them, the parents might be so entranced with him that they would push the two-year-old aside. So Monarch introduced the birthmother to families who knew each other.

She chose two families who belonged to the same church. They are close friends and visit regularly. The children call the second family aunt and uncle and they're very happy. The two couples stay in touch all the time and they write to and talk on the phone with the birthmother. She doesn't want to see them because she thinks it could be traumatic for the kids, according to Monarch.

At this point the birthmother doesn't want pictures, but they are available for her. Both families love her and would do anything for her.

"I went to the little girl's fifth birthday party Sunday and both families were there," Monarch added.

Pati's Story

Pati, a tall willowy blonde, was a client of New Beginning. I drove to Laguna one hot smoggy afternoon and we went out for dinner while she told me her story. She was 21 and living by

*herself when she got pregnant almost two years ago. She moved
back in with her mother when she was about six months
pregnant and still lives with her. She works as a secretary now
in a small business a few miles from her home.*

When I learned I was pregnant I had that feeling of total
frustration. I knew this was going to happen because I was
playing with fire. You know, that feeling when you want to
cry but you don't because you know it's your own fault.

I felt devastated and frightened. The baby's father and I
were still together in the beginning and we split the cost of
the pregnancy test. But after he found out it was positive,
and with me going through morning sickness and being
very demanding, he kind of backed out of the relationship.
I couldn't understand why, and it was awful.

But he did support me in the adoption decision. He
helped me choose the family but then he more or less
eased himself out the back door when no one was looking.

I thought almost from the beginning that adoption was
for me. My mother wanted me to get an abortion but I
couldn't do that. So first I called an adoption agency but
they seemed cold. Then one of my mom's friends told me
about New Beginning and I called them. Immediately they
said, "Where are you? How can we help? Let's meet for
lunch." So the following week on my lunch hour we went
out together.

Six Couples Interviewed

They brought a bunch of photos along with adoptive
couples' stories. But first they talked with me about what I
wanted and what I was doing. I looked through the
resumes and chose six. They helped me write up an
interview sheet. I wrote down everything I wanted to know
about the couple I might choose for my baby.

Then Jackie invited them to my house for interviews. I
wanted them there because I felt more comfortable there,
and I lived alone. Jackie always stayed with me while we
talked. Some I knew right away weren't right — the way
they were, their manner. For one thing, it was important to
me to have a full-time mother for my baby, but some of the

women who could afford to stay home planned to continue
working.

One of the couples turned me off because they wanted
one of those New Age babies who would be brilliant by
the time he was five. They had his entire education
worked out, almost the whole career plan. It turned me
off. That wasn't what I wanted for my child.

It's important at this point to be in control, to know what
you really want in childrearing, then look for it. It's out
there.

After I interviewed these six couples, I narrowed it down
to two. Then my boyfriend got into the act. He and I spent
a whole day with each couple. We didn't choose one
couple because the father never spoke. I loved the mother
but the father wouldn't share at all. I wanted someone who
could open up and communicate.

We spent the day at the swap meet with the other
couple, and we chose them. Ginny started taking me to
the doctor. She took me to dinner several times and we
were fairly close. She helped me when Craig and I started
splitting up.

Ginny told me she would like to help me deliver my
baby. I didn't see anything wrong with that. However, I
talked about it with the psychologist I was seeing. She
said, "If you were to change your mind and decide to keep
the baby, you wouldn't want them there. You want
someone there who has no vested interest in the child —
unless, of course, it's the baby's father."

So I let Ginny know I had talked to the psychologist and
that she didn't think it was a good idea. Later on Ginny
told me they thought my saying that meant I really wasn't
going to give up my child for adoption.

Adoptive Couple Backs Out

Then Ginny told me they were planning a trip. I called
them a few days later and they weren't there. I tried
several more times, then decided they must have gone on
their trip without telling me.

Finally, after a week, they called to tell me they had been
out of town. They said they would like to see me. This
was odd, these people who were so open and so friendly,

and I was pissed. I told them I was busy that weekend. Ginny called again Sunday morning and said, "I can't wait any longer. I have to talk with you." Then she told me a friend had told them about a girl who was having a baby and asked if they wanted it. They did, and they were in the delivery room with her. They already had the baby!

Here I was in my seventh month and my careful plans had fallen apart. Craig was out of the picture. I couldn't face those interviews again. So I called New Beginning and said, "You know what I like, what I'm looking for. I'm delivering in two months and I don't want to sit around and wonder who the parents will be."

So they sent me six more resumes and I picked two. The first one I called was really weird. She wanted my medical records right then, but I said, "Wait a minute, I haven't even picked you yet."

She Makes Another Choice

The other couple lived in Kansas City. I went over to the New Beginning office and Jackie called them. I talked with them for at least an hour. I picked them. Ray's a doctor, and they're great. They have a four-year-old daughter — that was one thing I really wanted, someone who already had a child. I didn't want them practicing on my baby!

I didn't meet Melissa and Ray until they came out to pick up the baby. The wonderful thing was they came in to see me first. They came into my hospital room with Janie, their little girl, and the father handed me a dozen long-stemmed roses. It was really special that they came to see me first.

Their little girl didn't know who I was. She must have been terrified because I know I looked like the wrath of God. She loves my baby. They say she dotes on him. When he got sick she couldn't go near him. So when her girlfriend came over to play she said, "I can't get near my baby brother and you can't either!" She wanted to name him McDonald because that's her favorite place to eat.

Melissa and Ray have written to me several times in the ten months since Robbie was born. They even sent me a lock of his hair. Melissa tied a blue ribbon around it and wrapped it up nice. I have it in my photo album.

They took care of everything I needed. I didn't have insurance so they paid my hospital bills.

They knew how I felt when the first couple backed out of our agreement because they had had the same thing happen to them. There was a birthmother back in Kansas City who had picked them. They had spent time together and had developed a close relationship. But the day before she delivered, her best friend was killed in an accident and she decided to keep the baby. They had been so close, and they weren't sure they could handle it again. So at first we talked through Jackie — I didn't have their phone number. Then after a while they gave it to me.

I had nine or ten counseling sessions. New Beginning paid for it. I had one in the hospital the day I left, and a couple after that. I never did regret my decision to release the baby, although of course I was sad at first. But I know that was the right decision for me and for the baby — and for the adoptive parents, too. I grieved, but it went away when I thought, what would I be like this minute if I had a child to care for?

The funny thing is I don't keep in touch with Robbie's family, but they do with me. I don't think about it a lot. When I see infants, I ask how old they are because I want to know if they're at his stage. Other than that, I don't think about him a lot.

I think it's because I was involved. I know where Robbie is, I know he's all right. Every baby I see I know is not him. Every set of parents I see I know are not his. I know where he is. I know what he's doing. I can talk about him with such love, warmth and fondness, and I don't feel bad. I can say how cute he is, how special, how blessed, but I don't have a longing that I should have him. I think I did the right thing.

Melissa and Ray's Experience

Melissa shared their experiences by telephone. She and Ray obviously have very warm feelings for Pati. In fact, Melissa said they're now trying to get in touch with their daughter's birthmother. Janie's adoption several years ago was totally closed, and now they'd like to have some contact. Melissa said:

We've been through years of infertility studies, both before and after we adopted Janie. The doctors can't find anything wrong.

We were so thrilled with Janie's adoption that it was not a second choice for us. We wanted to stop messing around with the infertility work that had gotten us nowhere. We adopted Janie in Ohio, then moved here to Kansas City.

I had found New Beginning's name in a *Newsweek* article — when you're infertile, you clip articles, save telephone numbers, addresses, the name of a friend of a friend who has the name of a good agency, any piece of information about adoption. I filed all this stuff away along with the brochures on how to fix the refrigerator and everything else.

I called New Beginning and they sent us an application. We also applied several places here in Kansas City. Janie's adoption wasn't open at all, but it was independent, and we felt comfortable with that approach.

Two or three months later Jackie (counselor) called and said they were giving our resume to a young lady. She chose someone else, but we felt encouraged that someone was at least looking at us. Then here in town a young woman selected us, but a few hours before she delivered, she decided to keep her baby. That was hard to handle.

Then Jackie told us about Pati. She explained that Pati had chosen another couple and had established a relationship, only to have the couple adopt someone else's baby three months before Pati was due. Pati was very upset about the other couple. She had made this huge decision and now she had to do it all over. I wouldn't have been surprised if she had decided to keep the baby after that.

We seemed to hit it off in that first phone call. I felt she was so sweet and so sincere. We talked a lot on the phone and sent letters back and forth those three months. She sent us photographs of herself, and we got basic information from the agency about Craig, the birthfather. We were relieved that he agreed with the adoption plan.

A week before Robbie was born, Pati called and asked if we had a car seat. "You know you'll need one," she said. She made a number of suggestions like that which showed how much she cared, how much she loved this baby.

She was very upset once when she called. She'd been to
her LaMaze class with her coach, a close friend of hers.
Pati said she was the only one in the class who didn't have
a male coach. She said it really hurt to go there every
week and see everyone else as couples. I felt so special
that I was the one who shared her hurt.

Pati called the evening she started labor and asked us to
get packed up. She wanted us to be there as quickly as
possible. We scheduled a flight out the next morning. Then
Pati called back about 3 A.M. Ray answered the phone and
she said, "Congratulations, Daddy. You have a son."
Needless to say, we didn't get back to sleep!

We called New Beginning from the Los Angeles airport,
and they told us we didn't have time to drop our luggage
at our friend's home. Pati was being discharged that
evening, and she wanted to know if we could take the
baby that night. We said sure, but that we'd have to find
some formula.

On the way to the hospital we picked up two dozen
roses for Pati. Walking into her hospital room was a little
uncomfortable because we knew she could still change her
mind. She said immediately, "Have you seen him?" We
replied, "No, we wanted to see you first. We also wanted
to give you the opportunity to tell us to leave." She
responded, "No, no no. You've got to see him. He's
beautiful."

Jackie was there. She, Janie, Ray, Pati and I all went up
to the nursery to see Robbie. He was magnificent, just
beautiful. As we looked in the window, Pati started crying,
and Jackie went back to her room with her. Pati was back a
few minutes later and said, "Have you asked the nurses if
you can hold him and feed him?" I couldn't believe they'd
let us do that, but they did.

Pati went back to her room to pack her things so her
mother could take her home. We stayed up in the nursery
area with the baby, and they let Ray and me gown up and
go in and feed him.

As I was giving Robbie his first bottle, I turned around to
see this man looking in the window. It was Craig, the
birthfather. That was kind of strange. Here I was, feeding
his baby. He was glowing, and he motioned to me to hold

Robbie up to show him. The tears were rolling down my face as I watched him.

After we finished feeding Robbie, we went out and talked with Craig for almost half an hour. I remember looking into his eyes, looking and looking, trying to memorize him and get to know him in what I knew was going to be a very short time. He must have reached out and hugged Ray four or five times while we talked.

We went to dinner, and by the time we came back, Craig was gone. Pati had signed the papers and gone home. We stayed at our friend's house until Robbie was eight days old because the airlines wouldn't take him until then.

We've kept in pretty close touch with Pati although it's tapered off a little this summer. For the first three months, her letters were all about Robbie. She went through post-partum depression, but I think the counseling she had must have been wonderful. She seemed to have worked out all kinds of things before she delivered.

I hope we see her again. I think we will.

We don't know Janie's birthparents, but five months after Robbie was born, I wrote to our attorney back in Ohio. I asked him to ask the other attorney to contact Janie's birthmother and tell her we're willing to send her photos and let her know how Janie is. Knowing Robbie's mother and caring about her makes us feel a little cheated for Janie. We hope we can be in touch with her birthmother too.

13

Teen Pregnancy Crisis —
Choosing Open Adoption

More than a million teenagers become pregnant in the United States each year, and 600,000 give birth. At least half of these young parents are not married. Yet only four percent choose to release their babies for adoption. Why?

Choosing adoption is always a hard decision for birthparents. Even when adoption was considered the "solution" to most too-early pregnancies, the birthmothers involved did not find it an easy, painless ending to their dilemmas.

Why Don't They Release?

Bonding starts before delivery. I didn't place any of my five children for adoption, and the fact that I was married and in my twenties is irrelevant. A 15-year-old mother has those same feelings of intense love for her child even before it is born. A 16-year-old mother of a five-month-old said, "I couldn't give my baby to someone else because she's a part of me and she needs to be with me! And I love her very much."

Adoption is not an easy decision.

Another reason she keeps her baby may be the simple fact that she wanted a baby. Some young women have little else. Others simply have the same desire for a baby that many older women have.

A 17-year-old whose child is 11 months old, wrote. "I didn't consider adoption because I wanted this baby. If I had given her up, I would have regretted it the rest of my life."

Pressure from family and friends is a big reason most teenagers don't choose adoption. A mother once said to me, as she pointed at her 16-year-old pregnant daughter, "I'd kill her if she even thought of giving that baby away."

Lupe, who shares her story in chapter 15, encountered a great deal of resistance from her mother and from her grandmother when she told them she was planning adoption for her baby. She reported:

> My mother and grandmother didn't agree with me. My grandma, especially, couldn't handle the fact that I was giving up this child. There was a cousin who wanted to adopt him which was grandma's way of keeping him in the family. I lived with grandma until I was five, and we've always been close.
>
> Grandma and I talked quite a bit but we didn't really communicate much — because she was hearing what she wanted to hear. She would cry on the phone and tell me it was almost killing her. I told her that if I made it through, she would make it too.
>
> My mother lived back east, and we wrote letter after letter. She would say, "I did it. I was 16 when I had you." And I'd say, "Look at what I went through. I don't want that for him."
>
> She would tell me all the wrong things about adoption. "Blood is thicker than water," she'd say. I would write back and tell her I knew what I was doing was right. He obviously would have a better life than he would if I kept him. I'm glad I didn't change my mind for them. But it's hard, very hard.

Lupe discovered that open adoption made it easier for her grandmother to accept the baby's adoption:

> After Shawn was born, she wrote to Steve and Kate and they wrote back to her. They have talked on the phone,

and now Grandma tells me I couldn't have made a better choice. I'm glad because that worried me a lot. Now Grandma sends Care packages to Shawn every couple of months — toys, clothes, newspaper articles about anything that might apply to Shawn.

Many teenage fathers are opposed to adoption. One young mother said, "The baby's father hates the word adoption. He'd never forgive me if I did such a thing." Yet six months after their baby was born, this young father dropped out of her life and started dating someone else.

It's not surprising that most teenagers do not choose adoption. Her parents tell her she should keep her baby, her boyfriend insists adoption is absolutely out of the question, and her other friends say, "How could you possibly give your baby away?"

Hard To Plan Realistically

The adoption decision may be even harder for very young birthmothers. Adolescents generally have trouble planning very far ahead. One reason so many pregnant adolescents keep their babies to rear themselves is because they feel it will all work out.

She may know that the majority of teenage mothers never finish high school and must depend on welfare for financial support. She may know that a big majority of teenage marriages end within a few years, and that teenage mothers who marry are likely to be alone again very quickly.

She may have heard that if a woman bears her first child before she is 18, 90 percent of her life script is written — she will be poor, she will never be able to get a good job, and she may marry someone she would not have married otherwise because she feels she has to.

But most teenagers don't think this will ever happen to them. Their developmental stage simply is not to the point where they can look far ahead and plan realistically for their future. If she is pregnant, she really believes it will all work out.

Over and over I see this kind of magical thinking in my class of pregnant teenagers. I ask students to make a detailed five-year plan. Often it reads like this: "I'll have my baby and then I'll graduate from high school with my class. John and I will get married and he'll have a good job. In five years we'll have our own house, two more kids, and I'll stay home and take care of them while he supports us."

With a script like this, why consider adoption?

The Historical Picture

We're told that about 80 percent of pregnant and unmarried teenagers in the United States released their babies for adoption in the 1950s. Today about 4 percent do so. Why the tremendous difference?

Part of the difference may be blamed on incomplete statistics. The 80 percent probably was based on Anglo teenagers. Most Black and Hispanic pregnant teenagers were keeping their babies to rear themselves. But the drop in teenagers releasing their babies for adoption has been startling. A look at widespread changes in our culture provides much of the explanation.

In the 1950s, the concept of the importance of the traditional nuclear family was stronger than it is today. The man was supposed to earn the living while the woman took care of the house and kids. She could not support her family. (Of course many women did, but we didn't focus on that fact.)

Teenagers in the 1950s were expected to be obedient and dependent, especially girls. The girl was expected to draw the line in sexual matters, and illigitimacy was a disgraceful thing. Because such a stigma was placed on illigitimacy and "unwed" mothers, it was important to keep such a pregnancy a deep secret.

A pregnant teenager was not allowed to stay in school, and her parents probably wanted her out of the house during this embarrassing time. Many girls were sent to maternity homes for the duration or to Aunt Matilda's farm in Nebraska. She was expected to hide out until she delivered, place her child for adoption, and return home as if nothing had happened.

The adoption was top secret — no one need ever know. Even the adoptive parents pretended adoption was exactly the same thing as giving birth.

Our culture shifted radically in the sixties, the decade of the flower children, the do-your-own-thing years. Teenagers became more independent. The sexual revolution arrived and the concept of illigitimate children faded. Material wealth was less important to some people. Adoption rates began to plummet.

The rise of the women's movement in the seventies made single parenthood more respectable. Abortion had a big impact on the adoption rate, and the sexual revolution hit the teenagers. Sexual activity among young people was on the rise, but birth rates didn't change significantly except among very young teenagers. The birthrate rose among women under age 15.

During this same decade, the adoption rates continued to fall. The secrecy of closed adoption no doubt helped cause the decreasing interest in adoption as a solution to an unplanned pregnancy. By this time, teenagers were exhibiting a great deal more independence. Peer pressure was more important than pressure from parents or other authority figures.

In the midst of all these changes, adoption changed scarcely at all. If a pregnant teenager considered adoption, whether she went to an agency or to a lawyer, she was not expected to be involved in her baby's placement.

A teenager newly into her search for self identity, into being her own person, was told she must not be involved in the most momentous decision she might ever make — deciding on the future of her child. To be involved, she had to keep that child. No matter that she was likely to drop out of school and survive on welfare while she struggled to raise her child. At least she was able to decide her own child's destiny.

Even if she is in charge, of course, the young mother who chooses an adoption plan for her child is making an extremely difficult decision. Few of us would want to return to the days when someone else made that decision for her, and she was told she had no other choice. Having choices is healthy, and for many teenage mothers, adoption, no matter how open and positive, is not the choice they will make.

Some teenage mothers are wonderful parents. Not everyone wants to be a "typical" teenager. Staying home night after night with the baby may be OK with her just as it is for many older parents. Some teenage marriages do succeed. So what is the solution from a counseling standpoint?

First of all, we must accept the reality of there being no one great solution for everybody. For some, perhaps many, there is *no* good solution. Being pregnant too soon is a difficult dilemma. Many teenagers "solve" it with abortion, sometimes at their parents' insistence, other times without their knowledge. Abortion is not an easy solution either.

Survey Of Teenage Mothers

In 1985, 131 students and alumnae of the Teen Mother Program, ABC Unified School District, Cerritos, California, responded to several questions concerning open adoption. Eleven of these young women were still pregnant, while the others were parenting their children aged one month to 11 years.

None of these young women had released a child for adoption. When asked if they had ever considered doing so, 18 percent replied affirmatively. Ten percent said they would have been more likely to release if the adoption could have been open with possible future contact with the child.

Almost two-thirds (63 percent) of these young mothers felt that the availability of open adoption might cause more teenagers to consider adoption, and another 18 percent either didn't know or did not answer. Only 18 percent disagreed with the idea that open adoption might increase the number of teenagers releasing for adoption.

Some of the survey respondents added written comments:

> Open adoption is a good way for a mother not to lose her child completely. The birthmother can keep in touch and that might make her feel better than not knowing how her child is doing. Open adoption might not make her feel so faultful (sic) for giving her child up.

> It depends on the person, but if I had a chance to have an open adoption, I probably would not have changed my mind at the last minute. (Young mother who planned to release her baby for adoption, then changed her mind after delivery.)

> All mothers want the best for their baby. It would be a lot harder to give your baby up if you had no idea of what kind of life it would have. If you could know your baby was getting the best, it could make both of you happier.

> I think it's nice you can see your child. But I think it will cause teenagers to consider adoption. And I don't think that's right to give your baby up, no matter how young you are or what! (Ninth grader who had to drop out of school to care for her baby.)

Pregnant Teenagers Face Difficult Decision

Teenagers who choose an adoption plan tend to be more independent and are more likely to have career and life goals than are very young mothers who keep their children to rear themselves. They can think ahead and can consider not parenting at this point for the good of their children and for their own well-being. Not all teen mothers have the ability to think of the future in this way.

Sometimes a birthmother knows from the beginning of her pregnancy that she is not ready to be a parent, and she decides an adoption plan is right for her and for her baby. The adoption decision is strictly her own. While grieving is almost inevitable for this young woman, she feels strongly that for her, and especially her baby, this is the best way to go.

Teenagers who choose adoption are generally interested in very substantial things about the adoptive parents, according to Sister Maureen Joyce, Director, Community Maternity Services, Albany, New York. "They don't care how they dress or how much money they make," she said. "They are much more interested in how much time they will spend with the child, and especially how much the father will be involved in parenting. They ask, 'Will he be home? Will he change the baby's diapers?' They are interested in extended families, brothers and sisters. They may not have had these things themselves, but they want more for their children."

For many young women, open adoption takes away some of the pain. Knowing where her baby is, knowing who the parents are, and something about their child-rearing practices helps her get on with her life.

Veronica's Advice For Teenagers

Veronica shared her story in chapter 9. She and the adoptive parents experienced a lot of stress as Veronica considered getting her baby back after she placed Katrina with the couple she had chosen. She finally decided adoption was the best plan for her child. She offered some excellent advice to teenagers, hoping this might prevent similar stress for them:

   If a pregnant teenager asked me for advice, I would tell her she needs to think hard about what she's doing. She needs to separate her emotions from her intelligence. If she has any doubt that she can take care of that baby or that she wants the responsibility, she should call a counselor and ask, "Do you know someone who has given up a baby so I can talk to her?"

   I think girls that age need to talk to somebody, and if there is no father to support them, they need to check out their resources. They need to figure out how they can give that baby what it needs.

They need to go to counseling before the baby is born —
I wish I had. Actually I think it would be a good idea for
the girls who keep their babies to go to counseling too.

So many girls keep their babies and say, "I'll do the best
I can." I could have said that, but I know darn well that
would not be the best for my daughter. I could buy her
food and clothes, I could work. But what if she came
down sick, terribly sick, how would I pay for the hospital?
You have to think about that too. Sure, you can go to the
county and ask for help, but how long can that go on?
That's not going to make you feel good about yourself. I
think girls really need to think about it and separate their
emotions from their minds.

This is the hardest part for pregnant girls, getting their
minds to open up instead of their hearts. While you're
pregnant, everything is so confused and you always have
somebody there who will hand out advice, somebody who
doesn't know the situation, who has never dealt with
anything like this before.

It's very hard to say I'm going to forget I love this baby
while I think about what I'm going to do. When you're
making these decisions, you have to remember you're
responsible for another human life. You have to think what
your decision will do to that human's life and that human's
mind.

Shauna's Choice

*Shauna made an appointment for an abortion when she
discovered, at 15, that she was pregnant. She thought it was the
only way out, and she thought her parents need never know.
However, her parents found her abortion papers, and absolutely
refused to let her carry out her plan. Shauna shared her story:*

At first I didn't think that was fair, and then Mother and
Dad came around and said it was up to me. So I thought
about it and thought about it for a month, and decided to
have the baby. I knew if I had an abortion, I would have to
deal with a lot of hurt.

Then I had to decide if I would keep my baby or put it
up for adoption. My parents said they couldn't afford to

help me if I kept it. My mom called around and found out about open adoption, and she called Claire (adoption service counselor).

When I first talked with Claire, I didn't know what I wanted to do. About two months before my due date, I decided it had to be adoption. So I went down and looked through all the files. There seemed to be something wrong with every couple, but finally I chose one and we went out to dinner, my parents, me and them.

Mostly I didn't talk. My parents talked with them. It was all right with me because I felt real uncomfortable at the time. Breanne and Eric were nice people, so I said it was OK with me for them to have the baby.

I didn't really think about it, about giving my child up. I totally locked it out of my mind until I went into labor. I wouldn't let myself realize I was actually bringing a baby into this world. After Travis was born I kept thinking, this is not my baby.

That first night the nurse came into my room and said the adoptive parents were there. Was it all right for them to feed the baby? I guess that was the first time I realized what was happening. After carrying the child for nine months, he is a part of you. After he's gone, there's nothing left.

After Breanne and Eric left, they brought Travis into my room. When they put him in my arms I just wanted to hold on to him. The next day when I left I signed a bunch of papers to release my baby. I guess more than anything in this world I would like to have Travis back, but I can't.

I think about him every day and wonder what he's doing, who he'll grow up to look like, what it would have been like if I had kept him.

At first I hated my parents for telling me I had to have the baby. I didn't want to do that because I felt like it would ruin my life. But I did make the decision. By law it was my decision and I decided to go through with the pregnancy and the adoption. I think if I had been 18 when I had Travis, I would have kept him, but I was only 15.

I didn't have much contact with Breanne and Eric until about three months later. My mom called them and asked if I could visit them. I thought I'd feel a little better about it if I could see where they lived. We went over to their house, and now I know Travis is all right. I'm glad I didn't go through another kind of adoption where I wouldn't know where my baby is and where I wouldn't have any contact with them.

When Travis gets older, if he wants to meet me, he can. I want to see how he turns out. I have to go through a lot of pain, but knowing Travis is OK makes me feel better.

Shauna's Pain Continues

There was no good solution for Shauna. She was pregnant and she, with her parents' urging, decided against abortion. She wasn't ready to parent. But carrying out her adoption plan was extremely hard for her. Perhaps more intensive counseling could have helped her deal a little better with her grief.

Before she delivered, her adoption counselor brought two girls to her house who had already released for adoption. Shauna said, "They talked to me about their feelings and what they had gone through. That helped me a lot, knowing someone's point of view who had actually been there."

After Travis was born, Shauna talked with her adoption counselor by phone a time or two, but had no real counseling. She did talk to her best friend a lot, and she felt that helped.

About ten months after Travis' birth, Shauna was able to report, "I finally feel good about it. If I had to do it all over again, I would do the same thing. I don't have regrets, just sadness."

She continued, "I think most girls are just scared. Some of my friends have had abortions this past year. Two have had their babies and both kept them. And those children are not having a very good life. Their mothers usually want to go out with their friends and party, and they leave their children with their parents. I don't think that's a suitable life for a child."

Birthgrandmother's Reaction

In addition to providing support for Shauna, her mother had to deal with her own grief as she lost her first grandchild through adoption. She commented:

> I don't think Shauna would have been as cooperative about putting the baby up for adoption if we hadn't gone with open adoption. I think that was the major selling point that convinced her she could still care for Travis, if only from a distance. She would know what happened to him. I think that's a very difficult thing about closed adoption, just giving something of yourself away and closing the door. I don't understand how people can do it.
>
> I felt very despondent after the baby was born, too. This was our first grandchild and I have always liked having babies around. I tried not to let Shauna know how upset I was because I felt I had to be strong for her. I think the only one who saw it was my husband. He kept his emotions all bottled up inside, but I think there was a lot of distress for him too.
>
> I wish we could have talked with other parents who were going though this situation. That might have helped.

Some people who hear Shauna's story will think she should have kept the abortion appointment. Others will believe strongly that she should have reared her baby herself. Still others would have recommended closed adoption as the only sane solution.

She and her family decided open adoption, while a difficult choice, was best for Shauna at this time. One thing is obvious — none of these decisions would have been easy for Shauna or for her family.

Travis Brings Joy to Eric and Breanne

Shauna's decision has brought a great deal of joy into the lives of the couple she chose to rear her baby. Eric and Breanne live in a nice little house in a Los Angeles suburb. They enjoy working in their yard, being with their extended families, playing with their kids, and the many other activities typical of middle class suburbanites.

Ten-month-old Travis, a bright-eyed red-haired little boy, went to bed right after I arrived to interview them. Ashley, 2½, stayed up most of the evening. When she got a little rowdy, her parents decided she should go to bed. She didn't agree. They got her up again and told her she could sit quietly on the couch. She played rocking horse on her daddy's knee, then sat in his lap. She likes to read and spent quite a while with a couple of books.

Breanne: We were having a problem getting pregnant. When I finally did, I miscarried. It was devastating, especially for me because I was the one that started my period every month and knew I wasn't pregnant again. It was hard. I cried all the time. I wouldn't go in a baby department, and I felt very inadequate. But it never occurred to me that adopting would make me any less of a mother.

We decided after a couple of years that we would like to adopt a baby. First I contacted all the state agencies and got the same story — that they have slow-learning or older children or you wait seven years. Then a neighbor told us her niece in Ohio was about to have a baby and that it would be placed for adoption. Did we want it? We said, "Sure."

Eric: We know now that out-of-state adoptions are harder than those done locally. The state had a preplacement guy who came out and told us all about the legalities of it from their standpoint. Basically he looked around the house and told us what to expect. Then we got involved with the county. Somehow they lost the papers and had to go back to the birthmother and have her sign papers again six months later. We had to pay the lawyer in Ohio twice.

Breanne: When the county studied us, they wanted to know if I dyed my hair and did we have sex before we were married! I was so afraid that I was willing to answer anything, so I told her I didn't dye my hair. Today I might say I didn't think it was her concern.

Eric: Our neighbor went back to Ohio a week before Ashley was born and spent some time with Alice. Alice didn't have any counseling and it was a very shaky situation. They warned us that she might change her mind at the last second. We planned but we didn't plan. We didn't bring anything into the house, no baby clothes, no furniture, nothing, until the lawyer called and said, "She's on the plane."

Breanne: Then my mom and I went shopping during the five hours before Ashley got here. That was exciting — but it was just as exciting when we got Travis. I had wondered if we would care as much the second time — we did!

For Travis, we went down the day he was born, and we got to feed him.

Effect of Open Adoption

Eric: We went out to dinner with Shauna and her parents before she made her decision. They asked us some questions about what we did and about our family life.

If I had to do it again, I would want to do it this way instead of going out of state. Because we met the birthfamily, we know what they're like and they know what kind of family we are. I think in a meeting like that you can tell something about a person's intent — not that she wouldn't change her mind, but that she wasn't being forced. They are real super people. Her mother was extremely supportive, let Shauna do the talking but showed they were behind her.

Shauna visited us just before Christmas. She wanted to know more about us and our home. She took about 20 pictures, but none of them were of Travis by himself. They were all of him with Ashley or with us. They wanted pictures of our family.

I said I didn't have any concern about Shauna coming, but I really had a lot. I was afraid she would fall in love with this little guy. I kept him up all day so he'd sleep when she got here. He went to sleep right before Shauna and her parents came, but he woke up while they were still here. But thinking she might want him back was obviously not on Shauna's mind. She didn't even ask to hold Travis. I asked if she wanted to, and she said yes. She held him for a few minutes, then handed him back to us.

Breanne: Almost everybody asks that question — "Oh my God, what if they come to the door and want the baby back?" They think the worst thing that could happen would be for them to want the baby back, but the very worst thing would be not even trying to have Travis for our son.

Another thing I like about open adoption, thinking of Travis, is that if it were me when I was 15 or 18, I would want to know what kind of birthparents I had. I think the more we can tell him, the better.

We've had a couple of people tell us, "Don't tell him, don't tell him." I know two people who didn't know they were adopted until they were grown, and one is going through therapy right now. His parents could have avoided that by telling him in the first place.

Eric: Ashley won't have the family information that Travis has. Recently some of Alice's family came out from Ohio. I told her someday I'd like to write a letter to Alice, but she said, "Just leave it alone. There will never be a relationship there and you have to face that." That's going to be hard. It's like handing one child a packet of goodies from her birthmother, and telling the other one, "Sorry."

The neat thing about open adoption is that Shauna realized that even though she was giving Travis up, she knew the kind of people we were, and she knows she has the option of seeing us again. At first we said we were willing to meet her and that she could see the baby once, but that was it. But once I met these people, I knew it would be all right. I don't feel threatened anymore. Shauna's not an outgoing person. She's very quiet, but she is such a sweetheart. We were so lucky.

Claire was neat. She made it clear that her concern was for that young girl. We went in and started asking questions — and she said, "You know, we're here to counsel the girl. We aren't here to give you a baby." And we understood what she meant.

Breanne: And that's really right. We went through a lot with the infertility, but I think the one who goes through the most is the birthmother. I think a lot of people would like to take the baby and never hear from the birthparents again. That doesn't make any sense at all.

14

Children's Home Society — "Old" Agency Moves to Openness

Louise Guinn, Director of Program Operation, Western Region, Children's Home Society of California, San Jose, does not fit the stereotype of the "old-time" adoption agency professional who is the last to move toward openness in adoption. During her 27 years with CHS, the state's largest adoption agency, Guinn has seen agency practice change from completely closed confidential placement to complete openness on request. In fact, she's been pushing that pendulum hard in its swing toward increased openness.

"It hasn't been difficult to shift gears," she commented. "I've been one of the pioneers and I'm a fighter. When you're in this position for a long time, you should be able to see some of the mistakes you've made. Openness with counseling can be very healthy for all parties in an adoption."

Kathleen Silber, strong advocate of open adoption, joined Guinn in 1986 as Program Manager, CHS, San Jose. Silber, former Regional Director, Lutheran Social Service of Texas, San Antonio, is co-author of *Dear Birthmother.*

Silber commented that she is finding a much higher percentage of families in San Jose choosing to exchange identifying information than she did in the Texas agency. In Texas, for the vast majority, the agency continued to be the intermediary after placement. "Soon it will be the majority here who will be participating in completely open adoption," she said.

First Open Placement in 1974

The first open placement through CHS, according to Charlotte De Armond, former Director of Public Affairs and Public Education for the agency, happened in 1974 because the birthmother demanded it. "She was 16, he was 17, and they knew they weren't ready to parent, but they knew exactly what they wanted in parents. They wanted to meet them before the child was placed, and they did. We didn't publicize the meeting because we weren't sure we should have done it," she remembers.

"Ultimately I believe all adoptions must be open," De Armond asserts. "Not that it will be easy, but we must accept the fact that adoption is different. Up to this time we have deluded ourselves on this topic. People have to get a different image of what adoption is."

The Adoptions Branch of the California Department of Social Services interprets state laws regarding confidentiality in adoption as applying after the adoption is finalized. California agencies may bring birthparents and adoptive parents together until this occurs.

In the early 1980s, according to Guinn, the CHS Board of Directors took a stand in favor of open adoption. For two or three years, meetings between birthparents and adoptive parents were arranged occasionally with the state Director of Adoptions being involved and approving each situation.

Then the agency's state-wide committee drew up guidelines and the decision was made to prepare written agreements specifying the contact desired by the adoptive parents and the birthparents. The guidelines approved the exchange of letters, pictures and phone calls. Birthparents and adoptive parents may meet without identifying themselves, or they may choose complete openness and exchange names and addresses.

The Changing Picture of Adoption by Charlotte De Armond was published in 1984 by CHS in order to explore concepts and attitudes across the United States on a wide range of topics concerned with adoption. The CHS position on each topic, including open adoption, was clearly stated:

> CHS enters into open adoption arrangements only when the nature and degree of openness is mutually agreed upon by the parties, and each party is comfortable with the plan. The agency acts as an intermediary in all such arrangements. Direct hospital placements are available to the parties who have effected an open agreement prior to the birth of the child. (p. 34)

When *The Changing Picture of Adoption* was published, about ten percent of CHS adoptions were considered open in some respect, but less than one percent had included the exchange of last names, addresses, and telephone numbers.

Wide Range Of Options

"Whatever both sets of parents want, we can work out for them. We go all the way from exchanging non-identifying information to meeting to on-going involvement," Guinn explained. "We work it out as an agreement before the child is placed."

In Guinn's Western Region, the agency places about 150 children per year. This number includes older, special needs, and foreign-born children, but more than half are infants born in this country, according to Guinn. In the entire state, CHS places about 400 children annually.

CHS leaders became more and more favorable toward offering openness in adoption as they worked with older children. They realized that these children often profited from contact with their birthfamilies.

As the agency worked more intensely with people in their post-adoption service, they observed problems which had developed for adoptees and birthparents. These apparently were caused by lack of contact or any knowledge of each other. This, too, provided a push toward more openness in adoption.

Search/Reunion Data Collected

In 1975 the agency prepared and distributed a pamphlet titled "The Changing Face of Adoption" by Charlotte De Armond. The issue of search and reunion was discussed from the standpoints of the adoptive parents, the adoptee, and the birthparents.

Included in the booklet were separate questionnaires for birthparents, adoptive parents, adoptees, and others interested in the topic. Open adoption was not mentioned. Results showed the majority of birthparents, adoptees, and adoptive parents would not object to either the adoptee or the birthparent searching for the other.

"As we worked more and more with people in the post-adoption service, we began to see the kinds of things that were missing from their lives and the kinds of things they wanted to know," Guinn said. "From there we went to getting social background information to give the adoptive parents. Then the social worker started writing a letter to the child saying 'I knew your mother and this was what she was like...' "

The next step for the agency was to let birthparents write letters to the child and/or adoptive parents which were given to the adoptive parents when the child was placed. The birthmother sometimes sent a gift along with the letter.

"We've had birthparents involved for a long time in the selection of adoptive parents for their babies," Guinn asserted. "Social workers used to describe several couples and ask the birthmother to choose the one she preferred. Then we started using photo albums. Once she heard about a family she thought she'd like, she was shown the album which illustrated their interests and lifestyle."

Next step was an exchange of letters between the birthparents and the adoptive parents. Then pictures were exchanged, and finally the meetings, when/if desired by both couples. Adoptive parents may be in the hospital for the birth. On-going contact between birthparents and adoptive parents is occuring.

"We see increasing numbers of birthparents who want this," Guinn said. "In fact, we're reluctant to accept applications from families who request confidential placement because most birthparents want openness. Some birthparents prefer not to meet the adoptive parents until after placement. The majority of our clients meet once, and some of them continue meeting.

Individualized Program Offered

"We offer an individualized program," Guinn explained. "We have a lot of fathers involved, not just the mothers. We never want birthparents to feel obligated to relinquish their children if they are not absolutely sure this is their best decision.

"We do need to separate openness from the practice that some groups are calling co-parenting where the birthparent is an active parent of the child. We are not doing that," Guinn emphasized.

Guinn stressed the importance of counseling. "Our clients are the birthparents and the children. We consider the adoptive parents a resource," she pointed out. Adoptive parents receive a lot of individual counseling. They attend workshops to help them prepare for adoptive parenthood.

Costs of adopting a child through CHS vary. There is a sliding fee scale according to income up to a maximum fee of $5,800. CHS costs for providing adoption service is currently (1986) $5,900 per child. Counseling for birthparents is paid through United Way, auxillary income, and private donations. This income also helps offset the cost of placements.

Statewide Trend Toward Openness

CHS offices across the state of California vary in their enthusiasm for open adoption, but the trend is statewide. Julia L. Richardson, Program Manager, CHS, Los Angeles, stressed the need to treat each case individually. Complete anonymity is the exception.

However, birthparents and adoptive parents adopting through this office usually share first names only and no address, according to Richardson, because this is requested by both parties. To date, in fact, no one has shared last names and addresses, but the agency would comply with a request to do so.

The birthparent chooses the adoptive parents and usually meets them, sometimes before delivery. Most babies were placed directly from the hospital in 1985.

"It takes a lot more time to work out hospital placements, but it's gratifying for everyone involved," Richardson commented. "The birthparents are happier, and it relaxes the adoptive parents. Somehow, if she gives the baby to them in the hospital, they aren't likely to think this mother is someone who will take the baby away from them. A birthmother in Santa Barbara had the doctor hand the baby to the adoptive mother as it was delivered."

The Los Angeles office has had one client whose housing was supplied by her chosen adoptive parents, but not in their home. "We don't want pressure on her to release her baby," Richardson said. "We take each one individually and try to work out the best arrangement while doing some casework with both sides."

While more openness is a statewide trend in CHS, Richardson pointed out that people are different in different areas. In Santa Barbara, for example, more adoptive parents seem to be willing to pay the medical expenses of "their" birthmother.

"The risk is thoroughly explained before they do it," Richardson said. "We also work with the birthmother suggesting that she should repay the money if she decides to keep her baby. She knows this is something we cannot enforce, however."

She described one adoptive family in the Los Angeles area who paid the $500 a birthcouple needed for housing during the last month before delivery. After delivery, they decided to keep their baby, and they immediately left the state. Several months later, they sent the $500 back to the adoptive couple.

Education Of Adoptive Parents Stressed

In San Jose, Silber is stressing the importance of the educational process in preparing adoptive parents for the openness wanted by the majority of birthparents. Potential adoptive couples attend three weekly sessions of three hours each. They take an intensive look at open adoption during these sessions.

Silber expects CHS to evolve into offering all of the options available in independent adoption plus extensive counseling. Some potential adoptive families are offering to provide housing, some pay pregnancy-related expenses, all of the things generally available to birthparents only through independent/private adoption.

Adoptive parents may choose to house the birthmother in their own home, with an adoptive family which is not adopting this child, or some other place. "We make it perfectly clear in these situations that the adoptive parents are taking a risk. The birthmother has not made a permanent decision, and they might not get this baby. If she should choose adoption, they would adopt her child. 'You have to realize,' we say, 'that this is a gift and you must be willing to take this risk. Otherwise it is pressure on her.'

"The key to the whole process of working with birthparents and adoptive parents is counseling. Open adoption can work well only with counseling," Silbur asserted.

Valerie's Story

Valerie, who placed her baby through CHS of San Jose, is tall with long dark hair and a dimple in her chin. She is without a doubt a stunningly beautiful young woman, as her daughter's adoptive mother points out. Valerie, who always wanted to travel, is realizing her dreams. She is getting married soon and going to Europe for an extended honeymoon.

Four years ago Valerie was 26, a graduate of a Bible College, when she realized she was pregnant. She and her boyfriend had split up a month earlier. She shares her story:

I tried to talk myself into abortion, but I couldn't do it so I decided on adoption. I had just been accepted into nursing school, didn't have a career ready to go, and didn't feel at all secure about making a living for two of us. My family was very negative about adoption and wanted me to keep the baby.

The baby's father and I were still talking, and he would have married me in a second. I didn't think a baby was a good foundation for a marriage and I had my goals and ambitions.

I looked in the phone book for an adoption agency, then called Children's Home Society. They were very supportive and didn't push adoption. They helped me explore all the options in detail, down to how much diapers and formula would cost each day.

As I thought about the adoption, I knew I had to meet the couple who would raise my child. It was important to me to be able to visualize where she would be. Back then, CHS was just beginning to get into the open thing. I told them that was my requirement. They had to meet me — not because I was going to tell them what to do, but for my own peace of mind.

I picked a family who agreed, but they got another baby the month before mine was born. I felt lost.

I talked with my social worker again, and looked at some other files. Then she told me about Jayne and Mark. They were exactly what I wanted and they were willing to meet me. They had another adopted child and had tried to communicate through the agency with her birthmother.

The day I was supposed to meet Jayne and Mark, I went into labor. I met them about a week after Rachael was born, and it was a very emotional event. In fact, it was the first meeting this CHS office had done, and it was a big thing for the social workers.

Jayne and Mark are extremely sensitive people, and a bond between us developed right away. They seemed a lot like me, and that was what I wanted for Rachael. The way everything fit together, I really believe it was meant to be, my not getting the first parents, and them stepping in.

At that meeting we talked about communication. They assured me they would send me pictures and letters, and they have followed through wonderfully.

They Meet Accidentally

More than two years later I was asked by CHS to share my experiences with a group of potential adoptive parents at their support meeting. I agreed, and when I got there, went into the kitchen for a cup of coffee. I knew an adoptive parent would also be speaking that night.

I looked up to see this person walking in, and lo and behold, it was Jayne! We threw our arms around each other and the tears wouldn't stop. We had both had fantasies about running into each other like this.

I gave her my phone number, and she asked if I would like to see my daughter. After some soul searching, we decided to spend an afternoon at the park together. Jayne, Mark, Rachael, her birthfather, and I talked, fed the ducks, generally got acquainted.

Rachael called me Valerie, but we were very distant at first because I couldn't believe this was the same little baby I had held in my arms. Was this really the same child? Yet she looked so remarkably like me. I was really taken aback. It was different. But we had a great time and I took a ton of pictures.

After I went home, I sat down and cried just to relieve the tension. The fact is I do miss Rachael, and I know what I've missed by not being her parent. But she has more in Jayne and Mark than I ever dreamed. Rachael is beautiful and I wish I were closer, but I'm glad she's where she is.

After that meeting, I came home and went back over the journal I've kept over the years. I have copies of letters I've written to Rachael, letters Jayne and Mark have sent me, Rachael's pictures — I keep them in this treasured notebook. Occasionally I lock myself in my room, sit down, and look through it, reflect, and think about it. I have a picture of Rachael up in my room.

I would like to stress that every time I see Rachael or get pictures of her or talk to Jayne about her, the more reinforced my adoption decision is and the happier I am with it. I think adoptive parents are so afraid the birthmother will some day change her mind, run over, grab that child, and leave. With me, that's not the way it is. Rachael has so much and I would never jeopardize her happiness. Each meeting I have even more respect for Jayne and Mark and what they have done.

Jayne has been very good about continuing to send me letters and pictures. I saw her and Rachael again last month. Jayne called and said they'd be in the area and suggested we get together. I bought pizza for lunch and took it over to the CHS office. We ate and played in the playroom there.

Rachael is a delightful little girl. She has straight brown hair like mine and my eyes. She doesn't just talk in words and phrases, she talks in complete sentences. She blows me away, she's so bright.

I expect to see Rachael occasionally through the years, although that's up to her as she grows older. She doesn't really understand who I am yet, but they are raising her with the knowledge she's adopted and that she grew in my tummy. I like their honesty and I trust their judgment.

I think Rachael may go through a phase some day when she won't want to see me. I'm aware that at any time she could choose not to want me to be a part of her life at all. That could happen.

I have found CHS to be tremendously supportive. And I like the way Jayne and Mark handle Rachael's adoption. Nobody wants to threaten her wellbeing or her security. There's sadness, but I feel comfortable knowing Rachael's with them. She has exactly what I want for her. She's happy, she's content.

Jayne and Mark's Family

Jayne and Mark, like Valerie, are tall. They live in a central California town in a ranch-style house with an enclosed back yard and swimming pool. Jayne enjoys her job as room mother for Nicole's class at school. She also takes her turn working in Rachael's cooperative preschool. Mark is a financial executive who insists on regular family outings for fun and fulfillment.

Although they had written to her through the agency, they had no contact with Nicole's birthmother until after Rachael was adopted. They appreciated meeting Valerie and decided they would like to be in communication with Nicole's birthmother, too. Jayne tells their story:

We had the usual infertility battle. We were married in '73 and realized soon after that having children would be difficult at best. I lost my battle with endometriosis, which necessitated a total hysterectomy four years later.

We applied for adoption to Children's Home Society in late 1975, but I didn't return the forms or follow through with their requests in a timely manner. My anger over not being able to have children like everyone else had to be resolved first.

Finally we were both ready and we applied seriously. We were in touch with them at least every other week. The social worker asked why we had waited so long, and I was quite frank. Apparently I'm not the first one to go through that anger. She assured me that it's important to resolve that before you adopt.

We only knew about typical closed adoption then. We were told sometimes there is communication from the birthmother, a gift for the baby, sometimes a letter. At that time we felt threatened at the idea of any identifying information being exchanged.

We adopted Nicole in '79 when she was 16 days old. With her came three blankets from her birthmother and a congratulations card to us wishing us much love for our new little girl. Her birthmother's youth really came through in that card, and for a long time it hurt me to read it. I felt for her so much.

The card was so significant because it identified her as a real, loving person. We didn't know her name, and I remember at the time feeling such dissatisfaction with the adoption process that made it end like that. I wanted to know where she was and how she was feeling.

We made a lot of inquiries. I know at the agency they felt it was important that we believe she was doing all right, but I never knew how accurate the information was. Everything seemed so beautiful that I wondered. I wrote her a letter through the agency and suggested that, if she were comfortable with the idea, she might communicate with us. We didn't hear from her.

We had this frustration when we applied for another baby. We said we were ready for an open adoption. We thought we were really geared up for it.

The day before Thanksgiving we got a call from the agency telling us that birthparents wanted each of us to submit an additional statement about our religious beliefs. I thought that would rule us out because we aren't together on this, but we were both very open and honest. Valerie and Ryan appreciated our honesty, and they chose us. We were to meet a week later, but Valerie went into labor that morning.

The following week, when we met with Valerie and Ryan, we faced the usual fears of rejection. I think, like any prospective adoptive parents, we had knocked ourselves out doing our notebook for the agency, trying to show ourselves at our very best. Of course we chose the most flattering pictures we could find. I was afraid that somehow we wouldn't live up to their expectations.

But it was a wonderful meeting with Valerie and Ryan. Their social worker and ours were also present. There were lots of tears and lots of hugging. They wanted us to understand their reasons for relinquishing Rachael. Mark and I came away from that meeting with great respect and admiration for both birthparents. I felt sad that these two people who we both liked immediately would not be a part of our lives for a very long time.

Then there was a period of waiting, about two weeks. It wasn't certain Valerie and Ryan would relinquish. Earlier, Ryan had considered raising Rachael himself, but Valerie hadn't gone for that. So we were very nervous. But they did sign and Rachael was placed with us December 23, our best Christmas gift ever.

For the first week or so I had a little trouble bonding with Rachael. She already looked so much like her birthmother, and I kept seeing Valerie and her loss. That troubled me, but the feeling passed because I knew both birthparents were OK. Mark and I loved Rachael intensely.

We continued to correspond with pictures and letters until we met 2 1/2 years later quite by accident at a CHS meeting where both Valerie and I were speaking. It was a wonderful, teary, emotional encounter. I asked Valerie that night if she would like to see Rachael. Then I went home and asked Mark how he felt about it. After some deep thought, he said, "Sure."

We met Valerie and Ryan at the park and Rachael, like many 2 1/2-year-olds, was real standoffish. It took her a long time, and she never did warm up very much. This disappointed me a little because I wanted Valerie and Ryan to see her at her best. But it was a good time and we took pictures.

She and Ryan gave us their full names and addresses that afternoon. When we parted, I was afraid I had made a colossal mistake. It seemed as though I had put a carrot up there in front of them, then yanked it back. We were moving and I didn't expect to see them again for a long time. I called Valerie and she said she was handling it fine.

The Other Birthmother

Several weeks later the agency sent us a sealed letter written by Suzanne (Nicole's birthmother) and addressed to Mark and me. In the letter she explained that she had not written earlier because she didn't know how we would respond. She sent us pictures of herself and told us a little about her life.

I called Suzanne the night I got the letter and we talked 144 minutes. She kept saying, "I want whatever you are able to give me. I only want what's good for Nicole." She also wanted us to know more about her and where she was five years after relinquishment.

Suzanne told me she is in remission from Hodgkin's disease and is currently being treated for leukemia. She appears to be getting along fairly well. I told her we would like to meet with her. I put together a bunch of pictures and other information about Nicole, but then I dragged my feet and didn't send them.

I was fearful because Suzanne's parents were always opposed to the adoption. If anything were to happen to Suzanne, we were afraid they might search for Nicole. At that point, more contact didn't feel right.

Six months later I called Suzanne and said I would send the things, but somehow I still haven't done so. But now I'm ready, perhaps because of the second meeting we had recently with Valerie. I talked to Kathleen Silber at the agency, and she said, judging from similar situations she's seen, there is much more risk in *not* meeting than there is in seeing her.

Kathleen feels strongly that openness is best, so Mark and I have decided we'll see Suzanne. We have relatives not far from where she is in Oklahoma, so perhaps we can arrange a trip there soon. We will want to meet her first, but I'm sure we'll get Nicole involved, too.

When I went in to talk to Kathleen that day while Valerie and Rachael were playing, Kathleen said to me, "I want you to know, I don't feel comfortable with ongoing visits unless the child is told who the birthmother is. She doesn't know Valerie is her birthmother, does she?"

She said she had seen families with younger children in meetings with their birthmothers, and the parents had leveled with the kids. They would say, "This is your birthmother. You grew in her tummy before you came to live with us and be our child." She said it worked fine.

Mark and I talked about it and then I called Valerie. Because disclosing to Rachael the fact that Valerie is her birthmother had not been part of our agreement, I felt that Valerie was entitled to some input into the decision. She said that would be fine. I waited two days to find the right time.

I explained it to Rachael as a by-the-way. We were talking about pizza and that tickled her memory. She mentioned Valerie, and I said, "Wasn't it fun? Isn't she a lovely person? Valerie is your birthmother and you grew in her tummy."

She looked at me and said, "No, she's not."

And I said "Yes, she is." And she just accepted it, particularly when Nicole began asking questions about her birthmother. Rachael then realized that her sister has a birthmother too.

I wouldn't in my wildest dreams have thought I could have coped with all this. The growth that takes place comes from the security of knowing that openness is not going to be disruptive. I advocate updating agreements with guidance through the agency.

Without our meetings, we would have missed the satisfaction of knowing our daughter's birthparents as real people and the reassurance and comfort that that knowledge will surely bring to our children in the years to come.

15

The Future
Of Open Adoption

Adoption in the United States is changing rapidly.

Agency after agency is beginning to offer some degree of openness in adoption, and some are helping birthparents and adoptive parents plan a fully open adoption with continuing contact.

The dilemma of adoption — are we serving the child, the birthparents, or the adoptive parents? In closed adoption, the reunion movement suggests that choice was made in favor of the adoptive parents.

Over and over birthparents and adult adoptees have reported their frustrations with the closed system. Most human beings who wish to be anonymous in an open society can generally do so. In a closed society, i.e., closed adoption, the choices are gone.

The irony of building the closed system on the perceived needs of the adoptive parents is that their needs do not appear to have been met. Time and again I have talked with adoptive parents with two adopted children, one adopted under the closed system, the other, with openness. They talk at length about the advantages of openness, of being able to develop a better relationship with their children because they no longer fear their children's birthparents.

CWLA Moving Toward More Open Adoption

The Child Welfare League of America, which endorsed confidentiality in adoption in 1938 and again in the 1978 revision of their adoption standards, formed a task force in 1985. People from across the country discussed current issues in adoption, one of which was open adoption. In 1987 the League will publish the revised *CWLA Standards for Adoption Services* based on recommendations of the task force and extensive review by national experts.

Joyce Strom, Deputy Director for CWLA, confirmed that agencies across the country appear to be moving toward more openness in adoption. "We're finding that more birthmothers consider adoption when they have some choice in the type of family and are assured of some information exchange and updates about the wellbeing of their children," she commented.

A member of the CWLA task force, Reuben Pannor is an outspoken advocate of open adoption. Retired Director of Community Services of Vista Del Mar Child Care Service, West Los Angeles, California, he points out that closed adoption removes adoption from the mainstream of American family life. In the mainstream, the blended family is becoming more and more typical. In fact, more than half of American families are divorced families. Children are dealing with two sets, sometimes three sets of parents. "We have learned to deal with these blended families," Pannor remarked.

"Let's say a woman is married, she gets pregnant, and the marriage breaks up before she gives birth," he continued. "Would we say to that father, after she gets custody, that he must have no contact with that child for at least 18 years? Would a court tell that father that he must pretend that child is not his anymore? Would a judge say, 'You made a mistake — your marriage didn't work. This child is not yours anymore and you must get on with your life. This child will be placed with his mother and when he's 18, if everyone signs consent forms, you can see him again.' That's what we have done to adoption.

"In the open adoption range there is a whole spectrum of choices. It's not a dogmatic thing, but it has to be open. To me, that's the direction and the goal in adoption. The sooner we move into that, the better our adoption practice will be, the healthier it will be. I think in ten years we'll look back on our practice of closed adoption and think we have moved a long way and learned a lot."

Open adoption is not easy, according to Pannor, because it requires people to have a whole different mindset. He says it was easier to think about adoption in the romantic light of providing this child to this wonderful adoptive couple, then forgetting about the birthparents. "It's going to take a lot of courage on the part of professionals to help educate everyone. Adoption means openness, adoption means humanizing the practice. It's a better system than the old one," he maintains.

Pannor described a situation in which the birthmother babysits for the adoptive parents on Saturdays while they go out. "They feel good about it," he said, "because they know the birthmother as a real person and she knows them as real persons. They know they are the parents of the child, and she knows that too.

"Why do we make assumptions that the birthparents are the bad guys?" he continued. "Birthparents are responsible people. They have an interest in these children and they want to do what is best for them. Why do we assume the worst? Respecting their child's birthparents as important persons in their lives takes nothing away from the adoptive parents. It simply removes the mystique of the unknown.

"Agencies have been locked into a lot of stodgy bureaucracy," Pannor commented. "They have made it very difficult for the adoptive parents, and they haven't even offered birthparents the help they need. They need legal help, financial help, and counseling."

Vista Del Mar welcomes anyone who is involved in adoption including those who have utilized independent adoption. "We are a social agency and we are expected to be helping people. We have a responsibility for those 70 percent which are independent adoptions. We're saying everybody can come here for help," he said.

A strong counseling program is offered at Vista Del Mar. Fees are modest, according to Pannor, and no one is excluded. There are no fees for birthparents needing assistance.

"Open adoption has to be synonymous with adoption. We have to get the whole profession to accept it," Pannor concluded.

Community Maternity Services Evolving Toward Openness

The change from the closed approach to openness comes about gradually in most agencies. As an example, Sister Maureen Joyce, director of Community Maternity Services, Albany, New York, described her agency's approach to more openness. She speaks of taking "baby steps" in moving from being an agency which "protected" pregnant women through anonymity to more openness in adoption.

"I think we've been slow in getting the whole delivery of adoption services to a point where we can look at it critically and ask, 'What is the best for this time?' " she commented. "What do our youth say? They say they have problems with adoption.

"Kids today have a say in the major decisions of their lives. They usually decide which college to attend. They plan their lives. But an adoptive plan for the child she loves is a far more important decision. We need to be very open concerning her rights and her responsibilities in this situation."

Sr. Maureen does not believe there is a set procedure to follow in adoption planning. "There might be as many options as there are kids, but sometimes it's hard for a staff to buy into this," she said. "If they do, they will bring the adoptive couples along with them. Often a staff needs as much education on this issue as adoptive couples do."

Records at Community Maternity Services have been closed since 1917 and they still are. Adult adoptees asking for information about their birthparents are given all the information in the file except the names.

Agency practice moved in the seventies to birthparents choosing adoptive couples from descriptions shared by the social workers. They were encouraged to send gifts with the baby, write letters, or prepare an audiotape.

For several years birthparents have been an important part of the educational process with prospective adoptive parents. Generally four birthparents sit down with five or six couples. Usually two of the birthparents are still pregnant, one has placed her baby for adoption and one is a single parent.

The birthparents tell their stories, the impact the pregnancy has had on their lives, and their hopes for the future. If she is considering adoption, she talks about what she wants for her child, what she wants the adoptive parents to say to her child about adoption, and why she is choosing adoption.

"That's a very powerful session for the adoptive couples," Sr. Maureen notes. "It's a rare group where everybody doesn't cry. I think it's the first chance for adoptive couples to verbalize how much respect they have for the birthmothers. At this meeting they begin to realize how important it is for them to learn as much as they can about the birthmother so they can share it with their child.

"On the other hand, the pregnant teens never knew before about the decisions the adoptive couple has to make before they decide to adopt. They are amazed at the whole issue of infertility, and at the procedures women go through in trying to have a child."

At Community Maternity Services, the birthparents choose the family they want from detailed descriptions. At this point (1986), they never meet or exchange names, but the adoptive parents write to them two or three weeks after the baby is placed. A few occasionally send pictures

to the agency and ask that they be shared with the
birthmother.

"I think we are on the brink of having them meet. For
some, this will be extremely important and satisfying and
will facilitate the whole healing process. There will be
others on both sides who find it very difficult," Sr.
Maureen commented. "I think we are on the cutting edge
of knowing what open adoption truly means and what the
effects will be. I mean totally open where each knows
where the other lives, and they have continued contact
over the years.

"In any good counseling you don't paint with a broad
brush. You treat each person as an individual. Some
people need more involvement in the adoption process,
while others know themselves and know they are better
off without it.

"I'm struggling, as someone who sets policy for our
agency, as to what is the moderate approach. I don't want
to be innovative and creative. I just want to offer the
flexibility that will meet the needs of the young women
and young men who come to our program. I don't want
the agency to be seen as the one that does all open
adoption or all closed adoption," Sr. Maureen concluded.

Dear Birthmother Has Impact

Dear Birthmother by Kathleen Silber and Phylis Speedlin,
published in 1982, has had a big impact on the growth of
open adoption. An adoptive parent with a bad case of the
jitters about "those terrible birthmothers" should feel
much more positive if she reads it. A pregnant teenager
who wonders if adoptive parents can possibly love her
child as she does may find reassurance in its pages.

Adoption professionals, judging from the many calls
Silber reports receiving from across the country, have
found the book a good resource for in-service for staff
members. It offers new insight to those determined to
continue the closed adoptions which allow them to retain
much of the power in adoption cases.

"When we first wrote *Dear Birthmother*," Silber says, "we realized the rest of the world hadn't gotten into openness much and we wanted to share our changes at Lutheran Social Service of Texas. We hoped to have some impact on the field of adoption. We had not anticipated how dramatically the change would come. I have been surprised at how many agencies have changed to more openness in the past few years.

"This has happened far more quickly than we expected in our wildest dreams. By the end of this decade, open adoption will be the norm rather than the exception. At the beginning of the eighties, it was the exception. The change has been dramatic."

Silber suggests that social workers sometimes become entrenched in traditional practice. "Agencies are like other social institutions — the change is slow," she pointed out. She recommends that staff members read about the positive results of allowing openness in adoption. Staff retreats in which they spend a day processing their feelings can be valuable.

"If an agency takes the time to educate its staff and look at open adoption in depth, it will be successful. If the agency simply says it will offer open adoption all of a sudden but doesn't sell the concept to the staff, it's not going to work," Silber cautioned.

"If the social worker thinks it's awful, she will not offer it in a good light to the birthmother. Of course we don't want the social worker to force the birthmother to meet the adoptive parents either. We want her to offer all of the options and then help that birthmother decide what *she* is comfortable in doing."

Cooperative Adoption

Cooperative Adoption: A Handbook by Mary Jo Rillera and Sharon Kaplan (1985: Triadoption Publications) offers more guidance concerning open adoption. Kaplan, a social worker for many years with Children's Home Society, Santa Ana, California, is director of Parenting Resources,

Tustin, California. After working in traditional adoption for years, Kaplan wondered why a child, in order to gain a family through adoption, had to lose her former family.

In *Cooperative Adoption*, Kaplan and Rillera offer guidelines for planning an adoption in which the child may benefit from close association with her birthfamily as well as her adoptive family. As an example, the authors describe an adoptive family with twin boys who remain very close to the birthmother and her family. The two families go camping together. Once when the adoptive mother and the birthmother took the two children into the camp shower room, a puzzled-looking woman asked, "Which one is the mother?" "We both are," they replied.

This family, according to Kaplan, became missionaries for awhile as they spread the good news about open/cooperative adoption. Then they settled into the naturalness of their situation and seldom come back to Parenting Resources because the members of the two families appear to be comfortable with the situation. They don't need the support of the group at Parenting Resources any longer.

"Social workers have said for a long time that family secrets make families crazy," Kaplan remarked. "Cooperative adoption is designed to prevent that kind of craziness.

"Cooperative adoption is not meant to be co-parenting," she added. "The adoptive parents clearly are the parenting parents and the legal parents. The birthparents assume the role of special friends or that of an aunt and uncle."

Various Agencies Offer Openness

The agencies and adoption services described in *Open Adoption: A Caring Option* are not alone in offering open adoption to their clients. All across the country agencies are becoming more and more open in their practices.

Carolyn Fowler, Adoption and Foster Care Supervisor, Fairfax County Department of Social Services, Fairfax, Virginia, reports that her agency offers completely open adoption plans. "We realized we must develop an approach directed at all three groups," she said. "Adoptive parents often fear birthparents, have never met a real live one. Our basic philosophy has evolved to where we realize that the more the birthparent can be a part of the placement of her child, the happier she will be with her decision."

Fowler described a 17-year-old mother committed to the Virginia Department of Corrections. When she delivered her baby, the foster parent went with the social worker to the hospital. The young mother wanted to keep her baby, but realized she had to hand him to the foster mother.

"This was a young woman whose parenting we feared," Fowler explained. "When she handed the baby over, she almost cried. The foster mother said later she had never realized what pain there is in giving up a child. Immediately this empathy developed which she might not have felt if the birthmother had not been part of the process.

"During the next six months we worked with the birthmother. We didn't challenge her parenting abilities or her determination to keep her baby, but we worked with her. When the baby was six months old she said, 'You know, I can't really take care of my child and that foster family can do more. I'll release if that family can have him.'

"This happens in our agency a lot. It seems to make a difference if birthparents know who will have their child, not just meet them for an hour, but spend time with them, knowing these adoptive parents totally care for the child. It works, it really works. Almost all of our adoptive parents want to meet the birthparents. If they don't, they feel cheated," Fowler added.

Lillian Earnest Gonzalez, Director of Adoptions, Christian Counseling and Placement Service, Portales, New Mexico, cannot offer completely open adoption because of her state's laws. They strongly encourage pictures and letters, however. She said, "Those pictures salve the wounds and give birthparents permission to go on with their lives. If, after somebody says 'You're terrible,' she can go back and read those letters, it will help. She doesn't have to buy into that garbage. She can go back and reassure herself through the letters."

Debbie Giguere, Single Parent Caseworker, Good Samaritan Agency, Bangor, Maine, reports that her agency is willing to provide open adoption if a birthparent requests it. Although they place less than ten infants per year, they are preparing adoptive parents for this eventuality.

After attending national adoption conferences, Giguere comments, "I think many adoption people are moving in the direction of openness. But one thing I have heard loud and clear, not just in Maine but in other states, is that the people who are not directly involved in services are more likely to be opposed to open adoption. More often, they say, 'Is this necessary?' 'Will this threaten the adoption triangle?' "

Situation Varies In Canada

If the birthmother chooses government adoption in Calgary, Alberta, Canada, she won't have a great deal to say about where the child will go. She may request a certain religious faith, rural or urban, other children, but these requests are not legally binding. Fathers' rights in Canadian adoption are much weaker than in the United States.

Betsy Young, Louise Dean School, Calgary, reported the usual advantages in private adoption — early placement in the family, opportunity to become acquainted with the people parenting her baby, possibly maintaining some kind of contact, and the ability to feel more in control. Nearly one-third of the students at this school for pregnant teenagers surrender their babies for adoption. More than half of this group choose private adoption.

Young points out, as others have, that the problem with independent adoption is the lack of a support network, someone who will be there when problems occur. Adoption is a life-long process. It doesn't stop when the adoption is final, it is just beginning. There needs to be support on an on-going basis.

Adoption laws in Canada vary from province to province just as they do from one state to another in the United States. It is important that both the birthparents and the adoptive parents fully understand the law concerning adoption in their state or province.

Suggestions For Birthparents, Adoptive Parents

If you are a birthparent and you want to know more about open adoption, call your local agency first and ask them how much openness they permit. Start by being frank with them. If you want to choose the adoptive parents and meet them, clearly say so. If you want to stay in contact over the years, tell them. You have the power until you sign adoption papers. You're in the driver's seat.

If you learn that agencies in your area are interested only in closed adoption, you may want to check on independent/private adoption. Be careful of the person who assures you he will "take care of you." You're trying to be in charge of your life, and an attorney can take over just as surely as an agency might. If you decide to work out an adoption plan for your baby, you want that plan to fit you and your child, not someone else. Say, "This is my life and my child. This is what I want."

An adoption counselor commented, when talking about open adoption, "All you need is one crazy among these four parents, and you have a problem." Open adoption takes a great deal of trust, and not everybody is trustworthy. If you are a birthparent and you somehow don't trust this couple, follow your judgment. Choose someone else.

If you want to adopt a child, and you would like to meet the birthparents, tell your agency. Ask if they have birthparents who want open adoption. If your local agency tells you they handle only confidential or closed adoptions, ask if they know of other agencies in your area which might be interested in your needs.

You, too, may decide to check on independent/private adoption. If you have a good non-profit adoption service in your area, check them out. Ask lots of questions. Be on guard with anyone who implies you are the primary client. The risk of adoption disruption is higher if the birthparent is ignored, put down or considered unimportant.

You also want to feel as positive as possible about the birthparents of your child. If you fear that birthmother, if you don't want to meet her, can't stand the thought of an on-going relationship with her, you may not be ready to adopt.

Whether you are a birthparent or an adoptive parent, before you decide to work with an independent adoption service, find out as much about it as you possibly can. Talk to other people who have placed a child or have adopted a child with the help of the adoption service. Are their charges reasonable and as specific as possible?

If no counseling is offered, consider the service high-risk. If counseling is provided, are the counselors professionally trained? What kind of follow-up does the service offer?

Know your own state or province laws concerning adoption. You can obtain this information by calling the state or province Department of Adoptions. A local licensed adoption agency should also be able to provide this information.

"I think independent adoption is all right for well-adjusted people. For some, it's better because agencies tend to be encumbered with bureaucratic red tape," commented Charlotte De Armond, former State Director of Public Affairs and Public Education, Children's Home Society of California.

"If you are doing it, I would have a contract drawn up that would include the lawyer's agreement, the birthparents' agreement, and the adoptive parents' agreement. The most important thing is for the birthparents to realize that the law says they are to know what they're signing, and that they're in charge," she pointed out.

"Try to establish with everybody that the key persons in adoption are the birthparents and the birthparents' desire to achieve the best parenting for their child," she continued. "We need to turn this around so birthparents can achieve this in a number of different ways.

"If the birthparents are not ready to parent their child themselves, they can plan an adoption. But in all cases, it is the birthparent determining who will do the parenting. If adoption is going to go anywhere, this is what we must have."

Lupe Chooses Independent Adoption

Lupe arranged her adoption placement herself, a risky way to go for most young birthmothers. But it's working well, partly because Lupe is a mature 17-year-old who knew what she wanted for herself and for her baby. One thing she did not want was to release her child to people she would never know or even meet.

Lupe had good pre-adoption counseling throughout her pregnancy because she attended New Futures School, Albuquerque, New Mexico. New Futures is a special school for pregnant and parenting teenagers. Lupe was involved in an Alternatives group which met two hours each week under the leadership of counselor Catherine Monserrat. In this group, Lupe was able to explore her feelings, talk about her options, start her grieving before she delivered, and anticipate the aftermath of releasing her child for adoption.

In New Mexico, agencies cannot legally provide completely open adoption for their clients. Lupe was not aware of any independent adoption counseling services in her area. When she decided she wanted to meet the adoptive parents before she placed her baby with them for the rest of his life, she realized independent adoption was her only option.

Lupe's Story

*Eight months after Shawn was born, I met Lupe. We picked
her up at her home, got in the car, drove out of the driveway.
Suddenly she said, "Wait, I forgot something." She rushed back
into her apartment and returned with her pictures — a full
album of Shawn at birth, at one week, two weeks, two months,
four months, Shawn naked in a little pool, Shawn on a horse
with his adoptive mother, Shawn sleeping, having his first bite
of spinach...*

I didn't find out I was pregnant until I was five months
along. I'd never had regular periods, but I finally went to
the doctor. When he told me I was pregnant, I decided
right away I probably wouldn't keep the baby. Adoption
would be better for him and better for me.

I assumed I would go through an agency. I talked to a
social worker several times, but it bugged me that I would
never know where he would be. So I thought maybe I'd do
it myself. A lot of people told me they wanted the baby
but it never felt right somehow.

Then a friend told me about Steve and Kate. She said
they were real nice, make their own furniture, create
leather pictures, and that they added on to their house
themselves. She also said they were very talented and they
liked animals. That was important to me because I like
animals. In fact, they used to have exotic birds.

They had waited 13 years for a baby. I made up my mind
that afternoon while this friend was talking to me. It felt
right, it felt like the right thing to do, and about a week
later we went out to see them. By this time I was six
months pregnant.

Steve and Kate live about 15 miles from where I was
living. From that first meeting it's gone well. I visited them
a lot while I was pregnant. Kate took me to the doctor and
paid my hospital bills. I would go over there and sit for
hours trying to let them see the baby kick. He would kick
like crazy when they weren't watching, then the minute
they looked, he'd stop.

Steve and Kate made plans twice before to adopt a baby,
but each girl changed her mind at the last minute. They

were afraid I would do the same thing and I vowed I wouldn't do that. There were times when I would break down but I knew I couldn't let them down. It was meant to be and there were no snags.

While I was still pregnant I asked Kate to come in and talk to Cathi, my school counselor. Cathi asked, "Aren't you afraid Lupe might change her mind?" Kate said, "Yes, but if she does, I have to believe that's best for her." She was totally relaxed. Cathi said if she had been in Kate's shoes, she would have been too nervous to make a good impression on me, but Kate was fine. She talked about how the infertility had been tough on their marriage, but she and Steve had worked through it and were closer now than ever.

I went into labor early in the afternoon. I was having weird pains while I was shopping with my friend. She said I was going into labor, but I didn't think so. Finally late that night I got a little nervous so I called my coach. We called the doctor at midnight and went in to the hospital. As soon as we got there, we called Steve and Kate. They said they'd be there first thing in the morning.

The doctor broke my water bag at 3 A.M. and the hard labor started. Shawn was born about 9 A.M. Jack, the baby's father, was there with me all through labor and delivery. We broke up about four months before I knew I was pregnant. We weren't friends at that time, but we became friends later and they let him in the delivery room with my coach. Jack was really good about it. He signed all the adoption papers, and I found out then that he was adopted, something I had never known.

The hospital wouldn't let Steve and Kate see Shawn — nor would they let either my aunt or my counselor see him. They said only my mother could get in — but she was 2000 miles away. Four of my friends came to see me and the hospital told them there was nobody registered there with my name.

Jack wheeled me down to the nursery. We sat in there for awhile and we both held Shawn. It was definitely a traumatic experience, the hardest thing I ever did. If it hadn't been for Cathi, I'd never have made it. I learned you have to cry, you have to grieve, that's part of the healing process.

Afterward it was strange. I came home from the hospital and was still kind of in a daze, just a tiny bit of denial. I finally broke down and cried and cried and cried. I can't even tell you how much I did that, but deep down inside I knew that was the best thing for me.

I went down to see Shawn every week in the beginning. It was real hard, seeing my baby with Steve and Kate. Even though that was my plan, it was still a shock. When I finally break away, it's going to be hard. There's a very strong bond between me and Steve and Kate, almost as strong a bond with them as between me and Shawn. They're great. I'd break down over there and they would say, "He's going to be fine." They've lived up to every expectation I had for them.

When I talk with Kate on the phone I can hear Shawn squealing in the background. He's talking now. He calls me Lupe. We still haven't talked about whether he'll know who I am — I don't know about that, but whatever feels right with Steve and Kate is OK. But I would really like Shawn to know I'm his birthmother, and I certainly want him to know he's adopted. He has his parents and he has me. That's the way it is and it's no big deal.

I think he was meant to be with Steve and Kate. As soon as I heard about them I knew I was doing the right thing. I was sure from the first minute — and I was right.

Steve and Kate's Experience

Steve Donaldson has sandy red hair, a mustache and a ruddy complexion. Kate, tall and slim, has curly black hair and dark eyes. They have a small crafts business which they operate in their home. They always assumed they would have several children.

They decided to pursue adoption. After Lupe chose them, they enjoyed a very open and close relationship with her — and still think very highly of her.

Steve: Thirteen years of waiting is a long time. We didn't try to have kids until we'd been married eight years, and when we did, nothing happened.

Kate: We had a lot of tests done, and the doctor finally said it was pretty unlikely I'd ever get pregnant. He suggested adoption, and we applied to the county. They told us about the three-year wait. We left our application, but we also talked to everyone. We talked to people at work, we told our family, our friends. We wanted as big a network as possible.

Steve: Not long after that, our doctor put us in touch with a young woman. We decided to meet in a restaurant. She described herself and said, "You can't miss me — I'm pregnant." I described us — "We'll be the nervous couple sitting in the corner of the restaurant." She was late and we were early which made for a long wait. We watched everybody as they walked in the restaurant — "That's not her." "Could that be..." Finally she arrived.

We knew she had to make a choice, but it really hurt us when she said, "I'll get back to you." We were there for almost two hours together, and of course we wanted to be chosen right then. But she had interviewed several other families and she wanted to mull it over.

So we set up another meeting. We had pads of paper all over the house. One of us would say, "I've got to write that down." "I want to ask her this..." "We'll tell her...about our family."

Kate: She finally chose us. She was already eight months pregnant so we didn't have long to wait. We talked on the phone a couple of times, but didn't see her again. Then she called us the day after she delivered and said she had decided to keep her baby. We were devastated.

Steve: Next time we met someone through my brother, but that fell through, too. She changed her mind about a week before she had her baby.

Kate: We were beginning to wonder if we'd ever be parents.

Steve: Finally a friend told Lupe about us. Apparently she told Lupe the right things because she came over to see us and said she'd like us to have her baby. We were excited again — and a little apprehensive.

Lupe's family didn't agree with the adoption at all. But she's a strong-minded young woman and somehow we felt this was it. We talked a lot, and it all felt right.

One reason she was planning adoption, she said, was that she had a pretty tough childhood. She was kept by a single mother and was continually handed back and forth between her mother and her grandparents. She didn't have a stable home and she wanted her child to have a better life.

Steve: Once Lupe decided she wanted us to parent her baby, we started taking her to the doctor, every appointment. She came over to our house several times. She wanted us to see the baby kick — we loved that. We believed she was less likely to change her mind after we bonded together. And we did become very close.

Up until this time we'd thought, "Aren't things tough for adoptive parents? All that time we were waiting, we didn't think about the emotions of the young girls. In fact, we were thinking it wasn't fair if she kept. But through meeting Lupe and going through the experience with her, we know what a tough decision they have.

Kate: The tears are real on both sides.

Steve: We got static from our families for adopting in the first place, and when they heard independent adoption, they were shook. We were amazed at the number of people who asked, "How much did you pay?" We paid Lupe's hospital bill and we hired two lawyers, one for her and one for us. We thought it was important we both have counsel.

Kate: We got to the hospital just before Lupe delivered. She wanted us to see Shawn right away but the hospital wouldn't let us until the next day. We've talked to Lupe's doctor since then, and I think they'll be a little more understanding the next time they have a birthmother who says she wants the adoptive parents in with the baby. They wouldn't even let her aunt in. Only mothers — no matter that Lupe's mother lives back in Missouri.

Steve: They finally said we could see Shawn just before Lupe went home. She handed us the baby and that was a momentous moment for us — I finally held our son in my arms. Our joy was tempered with Lupe's sadness, however. We told her over and over that she's welcome to visit anytime.

Kate: She came over at least once a week the first month or two. Being there seemed to help her deal with her grief. Somehow we weren't afraid she might take him back. I guess we had faith in Lupe — and deep inside, we knew that if she did, we would have to accept it.

Steve: But she didn't. She still visits but not as often. Shawn's birthfather visited once with Lupe, although they haven't been together since long before Shawn was born. Lupe didn't know until Jack signed the adoption papers that he was adopted too. He told us he wished he could know about his birthparents, and that he's glad Shawn won't have to wonder about them. For Shawn, his birthparents are a reality, people who loved him so much they let us raise him because they knew they weren't ready.

Kate: It still amazes us that we feel so close to Lupe — but on the other hand, she is Shawn's birthmother. If we didn't think highly of her, what would that say about our feelings for our son?

Lupe, Steve and Kate, three people who love Shawn very much and who want the best for him, chose to stay in contact. All feel Shawn is ahead if he knows both his birthparents and the "real" parents with whom he lives.

Lupe, Steve, and Kate, and the other birthparents and adoptive parents who share their stories in this book had a common goal: to make the best possible adoption plan for their children, whether those children are theirs by birth or by adoption. They looked at the problems associated with closed adoption and decided they needed a different choice. They chose open adoption — the choice where no one loses everything, and everyone may win.

Annotated Bibliography

Many books have been written for people wanting to adopt a child, for adoptive couples, and for their adopted children. Much less is available for birthparents, and very little in the literature is primarily concerned with open adoption.

The following list is limited to books which either deal primarily with open adoption or include information on the topic. With one exception, these materials have been published since 1980. Journal articles are not included, but two newsletter sources are listed.

The National Adoption Center, 1218 Chestnut Street, Philadelphia, Pennsylvania, 19107, is an excellent resource for anyone researching adoption. This is a library and information exchange which deals with special needs of adoption and also covers the gamut of adoption literature, according to Sharon Geiger, Information Specialist. The Center is financially supported through fund-raising activities and through grants. Phone (215) 925-0200.

Prices quoted for the following books are from *Books in Print*, 1986. Because prices change so rapidly, however, and because publishers move, it is wise to call your local library reference department for an updated price and address before ordering a book. Most publishers add a handling charge of $1.50-$2.00 for books ordered by mail.

Aigner, Hal. *Adoption in America: Coming of Age*. 1986: Paradigm Press, 127 Greenbrae Boardwalk, Greenbrae, CA 94904. Paper. 208 pages. $8.95.

Many of the problems in adoption policies and procedures have occurred because of the secrecy surrounding adoption, according to

Aigner. In this book he documents and analyzes the major
challenges faced in reform efforts. He is concerned with the interests
of adoptees, their birthparents, and their adoptive parents. He also
provides a fascinating and detailed look at the history of adoption in
the United States.

Anderson, Carole, Lee Campbell, and Mary Anne Manning Cohen.
*Choices, Chances, Changes: A Guide to Making an Informed Choice About
Your Untimely Pregnancy.* 1981: CUB, Inc., P.O. Box 573, Milford, MA
01757. 63 pages. $5.00.

Book offers constructive suggestions for questions a young person
should ask if she approaches an adoption agency for help. Mainly, it
is a reassuring booklet for young mothers who want to keep their
babies to rear themselves, young mothers who may wonder if they
can cope with the task of parenting.

Arms, Suzanne. *To Love and Let Go.* 1983: Alfred A. Knopf, New York.
Hardcover, 228 pages. $14.95

Presents the stories of several young women who release their
babies for adoption and of the parents these birthmothers choose.
Arms' emphasis is on the needs of the birthmothers and of the
positive effects of adoptive parents and birthparents meeting and
developing a relationship.

Brandsen, Cheryl Kreykes, M.S.W. *A Case for Adoption: A Guide to
Presenting the Option of Adoption.* 1985. Bethany Christian Services,
901 Eastern N.E., Grand Rapids, MI 49503. 48 pages. $2.00,
50+/$1.50.

Well-written booklet designed for counselors who work with
pregnant teenagers. It stresses respect and caring concern for
birthparents, and does not suggest that adoption is the only option a
young person could or should choose. Rather, it addresses the
concerns and frustrations counselors have expressed about
representing adoption as a loving, responsible, and mature choice
that must be considered as seriously as parenting or marriage. The
booklet presents a positive approach toward open adoption.

De Armond, Charlotte. *The Changing Picture of Adoption.* 1984: The
Children's Home Society of California, 2727 West Sixth Street, Los
Angeles, Ca., 90057. Paper, 144 pages. $14.95.

Based on extensive interviewing, mostly of adoption professionals,
this book gives information and opinions on current developments
and trends in adoption in the United States. It addresses a wide

variety of topics including independent versus agency adoption, open versus confidential adoption, adoption disruptions, open versus closed records, and other sometimes controversial adoption issues.

Friends in Adoption Newsletter. Dawn Smith-Pliner, Friends in Adoption, Box 87, Pawlet, Vt., 05761. $15 annual membership includes four newsletters per year.

Newsletter focuses on independent adoption as a viable method of family building. The group works for political and social reforms in the adoption scene, advocates for birthparents, and educates the public and potential adoptors about adoption alternatives including open adoption.

Gilman, Lois. *The Adoption Resource Book.* 1984: Harper and Row Publishers, Inc., 10 East 53rd Street, New York, NY 10022. 318 pages. Paper, $6.95. Hardcover, $16.95.

This very comprehensive guide to adoption is aimed at potential adoptive parents. Includes positive descriptions of independent as well as agency adoption. Also included is a brief account of open adoption and the advantages associated with openness. A state-by-state Domestic Adoption Directory lists nearly a thousand agencies along with names and addresses of parent groups, exchanges, public service offices, and other valuable sources.

Rappaport, Bruce, Victorie McEvoy, and Joanne Huddleston. "Adoption Is a Loving Option". Independent Adoption Center. 3313 Vincent Road, Suite 202, Pleasant Hill, CA 94523. 14 pages. Free.

A very positive pamphlet explaining independent adoption.

Johnston, Patricia Irwin. *An Adoptor's Advocate.* 1984: Perspectives Press, 905 West Wildwood Ave., Fort Wayne, IN 46807. Paper. 84 pages. $6.95.

Book focuses on the issues adoptive couples need to deal with as they plan family building through adoption. Author mentions open adoption briefly and provides a good discussion of society's feelings about adoption.

Johnston, Patricia Irwin, Ed. *Perspectives on a Grafted Tree.* 1983; Perspectives Press, Hardcover. 144 pages. $12.95.

A beautiful collection of poems written by birthparents, adoptees, adoptive parents, and extended family members. They express a wide variety of both positive and negative feelings which are part of the gains and losses, happiness and pain felt by all those touched by adoption.

Kirk, David H. *Adoptive Kinship: A Modern Institution in Need of Reform.* 1981, rev. 1985. Ben-Simon Publications, P.O. Box 2124, Port Angeles, WA 98362. 184 pages. $15.95.

Review of the background for the current controversy concerning the civil rights of adopted persons. Kirk shows that the difficulties peculiar to adoptive family life stem from well-meant but mistaken laws and administrative practices. He suggests new directions for adoption, both as human relationships and as a social institution.

Lindsay, Jeanne Warren. *Pregnant Too Soon: Adoption Is an Option.* 1980, 208 pages, Paper, $6.95. Rev. 1987. Pap. $9.95. HC, $15.95. Morning Glory Press, Inc., 6595 San Haroldo Way, Buena Park, CA 90620.

Young women who were, by their own admission, "pregnant too soon," tell their stories. Most made the unpopular decision to release for adoption. They share their reasons for doing so. Included with the personal stories is information on agency and independent adoption, fathers' rights, dealing with grief, and other aspects of adoption. Especially written for young birthmothers, but may also give adoptive parents added empathy for these young people.

Parents for Private Adoption Newsletter. Margaret Hutchison-Betts, Parents for Private Adoption, P.O. Box 7, Pawlet, VT 05761. Sample newsletter, $5.00. Organization membership, $10 year.

Through its newsletter, this national adoption support group helps people understand adoption issues and the adoption options available. One annual "Reader" plus four newsletters are produced each year.

Post Adoption Center for Research and Education (PACER). "Dialogue for Understanding I and II". 860 Bryant Street, Palo Alto, CA 94301. $7.50 each.

PACER serves all members of the adoption triad through support groups and education. These publications offer first hand accounts of the life-long impact of adoption from the personal perspective of adoptive parents, adopted persons, and birthparents.

Powledge, Fred. *The New Adoption Maze and How to Get Through It.* 1985: The C.V. Mosby Company, 11830 Westline Industrial Drive, St. Louis, MO 63146. Hardcover. 322 pages. $15.95.

Powledge discusses recent changes in adoption. One chapter, "Open Adoption and the Future," describes several agencies which offer open adoption, including some not featured in *Open Adoption: A Caring Option*. He refers to the "phenomenon called open adoption" and writes that many see it as an important part of the future of adoption. "At the very least, it is something that prospective adoptors should know about and consider as they start their journey through the system."

Rillera, Mary Jo, and Sharon Kaplan. *Cooperative Adoption: A Handbook*. 1984: Triadoption Publications, P.O. Box 638, Westminster, CA 92684. 158 pages. Paper. $14.95.

Offers excellent guidelines for birthparents and adoptive parents planning an open adoption. Authors do not recommend co-parenting except in the sense of both sets of parents being actively involved with the child. The adoptive parents are the legal and psychological day-to-day parents, but the birthparents may be as close to the adoptive family as desired by everyone involved. Suggested cooperative adoption documents are included.

Silber, Kathleen, and Phylis Speedlin. *Dear Birthmother, Thank You for Our Baby*. 1983: Corona Publishing Company, 1037 S. Alamo, San Antonio, TX 78210. Paper. 192 pages. $7.95.

A beautiful description of the advantages of open adoption to everyone concerned in the triangle — adoptive parents as well as birthparents and adoptees. Refutes what the authors call the four myths of adoption: 1. "The birthmother obviously doesn't care about her child or she wouldn't have given him away." 2. "Secrecy in every phase of the adoption process is necessary to protect all parties." 3. "Both the birthmother and birthfather will forget about their unwanted child." 4. "If the adoptee really loved his adoptive family, he would not have to search for his birthparents."

Sorosky, Arthur, M.S., Annette Baran, M.S.W., Reuben Pannor, M.S.W. *The Adoption Triangle: The Effects of the Sealed Record on Adoptees, Birth Parents, and Adoptive Parents*. 1978: Anchor Press/Doubleday, Garden City, NY. Hardcover. 256 pages. $8.95.

Authors re-evaluate adoption policies. Interviews and correspondence with hundreds of adoptees, birthparents, and adoptive parents are utilized to get at the central problems and issues. They suggest a need to reform attitudes and policies regarding adoption.

About The Author

Jeanne Warren Lindsay has worked closely with hundreds of teenagers during the past fifteen years. She is resource specialist/teacher for the Teen Mother Program, ABC Unified School District, Cerritos, California. Lindsay started the Program in 1972 as a choice for pregnant teenagers who do not wish to remain in the regular classroom during pregnancy.

Ms. Lindsay has advanced degrees in home economics and anthropology. She is a member of the Board of Directors of the National Organization on Adolescent Pregnancy and Parenthood, and editor of the *NOAPP Network*. She frequently gives presentations on adoption, the culture of school-age parents, teenage marriage, educating pregnant and parenting teens, and other topics.

Other books by Ms. Lindsay include *Pregnant Too Soon: Adoption Is an Option, Teens Parenting: The Challenge of Babies and Toddlers, Teenage Marriage: Coping with Reality, Teens Look at Marriage: Rainbows, Roles and Reality,* and *Do I Have a Daddy? A Story About a Single-Parent Child.*

She and Bob have been married for 35 years. Their five children include Pati, cross-country driver and owner/operator of an 18-wheeler truck; Erin, a political activist; Steve, printing company owner/operator; Eric, businessman; and Mike, an attorney. Bob and Jeanne have three lovely daughters-in-law, Kathi, Kim, and Tammy, one grandson, Travis, and are expecting more grandchildren.

Index

MAIL ORDER FORM

Open Adoption — A Caring Option
Trade, $9.95. Cloth, $15.95.

Other Books by Jeanne Lindsay

Pregnant Too Soon: Adoption Is an Option
For pregnant teenagers, parents, and counselors.
Many quotes from birthmothers.
Teens Parenting: The Challenge of Babies and Toddlers
How-to-parent book based on interviews with school-age
mothers who are quoted extensively. Easy reading.
Teenage Marriage: Coping with Reality
Marriage book especially for teenagers. Based on survey of 3,000
teenagers' attitudes toward marriage. Many quotes.
Teens Look at Marriage: Rainbows, Roles and Reality
In-depth coverage of research behind *Teenage Marriage*. Provides
insight into world of teenage couples.
Do I Have a Daddy? A Story about a Single-Parent Child
Picture story for child whose parents never married.
Includes 12-page section of suggestions for single parents.

Teacher's Guide and Student Study Guide available for each book.
For information on future publications and quantity price discounts,
please send for free catalog.

MORNING GLORY PRESS

6595-B San Haroldo Way, Buena Park, CA 90620

Quantity		Price	Total
	Open Adoption — A Caring Option		
_____	Paper, ISBN 0-930934-23-7	$9.95	_____
_____	Cloth, ISBN 0-930934-22-9	$15.95	_____
	Pregnant Too Soon: Adoption Is an Option		
_____	Paper, ISBN 0-930934-25-3	$9.95	_____
_____	Cloth, ISBN 0-930934-26-1	$15.95	_____
	Teens Parenting: The Challenge of Babies and Toddlers		
_____	Paper, ISBN 0-930934-06-7	$9.95	_____
_____	CLoth, ISBN 0-930934-07-5	$14.95	_____
	Teenage Marriage: Coping with Reality		
_____	Paper, ISBN 0-930934-11-3	$8.95	_____
_____	Cloth, ISBN 0-930934-12-1	$14.95	_____
	Teens Look at Marriage; Rainbows, Roles and Reality		
_____	Paper, ISBN 0-930934-15-6	$9.95	_____
_____	Cloth, ISBN 0-930934-16-4	$15.95	_____
	Do I Have a Daddy?		
_____	Paper, ISBN 0-930934-17-2	$3.95	_____
_____	Cloth, ISBN 0-930934-10-5	$7.95	_____

Also available — Teacher's Guides and Student
Study Guides for above books.

Quantity Discounts Available

TOTAL
Please add postage, 1-3 books, $1.50; 4+, 50c/book. _____
California residents add 6% sales tax _____
TOTAL ENCLOSED _____

NAME _____

ADDRESS _____